asic Cubase SX *D*

D0995808

051110

112255

Printed and bound in Great Britain by Antony Rowe Limited, Chippenham, Wiltshire

Published in the UK by SMT, an imprint of Sanctuary Publishing Limited, Sanctuary House, 45-53 Sinclair Road, London W14 0NS, United Kingdom

www.sanctuarypublishing.com

Cover artwork courtesy of Steinberg Media Technologies AG

While the publishers have made every reasonable effort to trace the copyright owners for any or all of the photographs in this book, there may be some omissions of credits, for which we apologise.

ISBN: 1-86074-565-2

basic Cubase SX

Michael Prochak

smt

CONTENTS

INTRODUCTION AND OVERVIEW

For practising musicians, producers and enthusiasts, Cubase has become one of the best-known music-production applications available throughout the world. Steinberg's latest release of this popular application, Cubase SX, represents a totally new generation in music-creation and -production software tools. Steinberg has spent more than 15 years creating the tools that musicians want to use, and all the best and latest technology is crammed into this all-new edition, Cubase SX. With SX's forerunners, Steinberg proved that, in an increasingly digital environment, there is no compelling need to keep shelling out for expensive and constantly out-of-date dedicated audio hardware in order to create extremely capable and creative audio workstations. Most users will find that Cubase SX is not just equal to most other available digital systems, but that it's one which, for a lot of musicians and producers, can actually be better, more comfortable and certainly more flexible. For example, Cubase SX comes complete with VST System Link, allowing several computers to be linked together and actually perform as one fully integrated system. This means that the idea of a maximum (read 'limited') project size simply doesn't apply any more. And it doesn't stop there.

As you get acquainted with Cubase SX, you'll find myriad advantages that give you unprecedented freedom to work in the way that you, the musician, really want to work. Features range from advanced automated mixing facilities with support for VST 2.0 plug-ins and virtual instruments and ASIO 2.0-compatible audio hardware to extremely flexible multiple undo and redo options, giving you the facility to selectively remove or modify applied audio processing at any point in the data's history. You have complete surround-sound support and handling that makes other systems look like such a facility was some sort of afterthought rather than an integral part of the initial design goal.

Overview

So what's new and different in Cubase SX? Well, basically, *everything*. Cubase SX is not merely an updated version of Cubase VST; it has been completely redesigned from the inside out. Fortunately, most of this is totally transparent to the user, and all of the main working areas of the program are still very similar to earlier versions. However, there are various changes in how recorded files are handled, there are changes in terminology used and the main menu structure is different, along with other cosmetic developments. But while these changes might make things slightly confusing initially to users of previous versions of Cubase, in the long run the advantages they provide make them all worthwhile.

What's Different In SX?

Although Steinberg has created a completely new application with the release of SX, to experienced Cubase users a lot of the look and feel remains the same, just a lot slicker and perhaps even a bit more intuitive. However, there are a number of distinct differences in SX that set it apart from previous versions of Cubase. These include:

Songs And Arrangements

Unlike Cubase VST, in SX the basic concept of songs and arrangements is no longer used. Instead, the native document format a 'project' (extension .cpr) is used, and all settings and file references relating to the project are stored in the Project folder, which is designated when you create a project. You can have several open projects, but only one can be active at any one time. You can, of course, work with multiple arrangements in the same way as on previous versions of Cubase, since several projects can share the same

Project folder. However, having different formats for songs and arrangements is redundant since you can now simply create new projects and assign them to the same Project folder.

Project Window Versus Arrange Window

The main working area in Cubase SX, the Project window, performs pretty much the same function as the Arrange window did in earlier versions of Cubase. This area allows for real-time placement of audio, video and MIDI parts and the performing of almost all primary editing tasks, including automation, as well as giving you an overview of an entire project. However, you will notice that Cubase SX uses different terminology to earlier Cubase versions for referencing audio files in a project.

Audio Channels

In the new version of SX, you don't have to specify the number of audio channels to use in a project, nor do you have to designate an audio channel to record on; you can simply create as many audio tracks as you feel you need in any project, a number limited only by what your computer can handle. For convenience, in Cubase SX an audio track and an audio channel are the same thing and all audio tracks will have a corresponding audio-channel strip in the Mixer.

Recording Audio

In earlier versions of Cubase, recording normally took place on the track that was selected. In Cubase SX, however, you simply have to activate the Record Enable button for each track on which you wish to record. The number of tracks on which you can record at a time depends on the number of activated inputs on your audio hardware. You can also set things up so that, on selected tracks, Record Enable is activated automatically.

Events And Parts

In Cubase SX, audio events can appear directly on audio tracks in the Project window, so there is no longer any need for audio parts. You can also put one or several audio events into an audio part, which is particularly useful when it comes to grouping events together and moving them all as one unit.

Dynamic Events

Sorry, there are no dynamic events for audio events any more. Instead, you now need to use the regular automation features to automate volume and pan. The matchpoints feature in previous versions of Cubase has also been replaced by a comprehensive hitpoint-editing feature.

Applying Processing

In Cubase SX, you can of course still use plug-in effects

in real time, but you can now also permanently apply the effect processing to selected audio events.

MIDI-Related Differences
Recording MIDI
As I said, in previous versions of Cubase, MIDI recording normally happened on a selected track, whereas in Cubase SX you can record on all tracks that are record enabled and set things up so that selected tracks are automatically record enabled. Unlike the MIDI input in previous versions, which was a global setting for all tracks, in Cubase SX tracks can be set separately for each MIDI track.

Setting MIDI Thru
In order to be able to play a connected MIDI instrument in Cubase SX, MIDI Thru must first be activated, which is now achieved either by record-enabling the track or by clicking the track's Monitor button.

Editing MIDI
In previous versions of Cubase, you could select a MIDI track in the Track list and open it in a MIDI editor. In Cubase SX, you need to select one or several parts on the track before you can open a MIDI editor.

Play Parameters
Cubase SX now extends considerably the potential for

real-time processing of MIDI data and comes with a number of MIDI effect plug-ins capable of transforming the MIDI output from a track in various ways. However, unlike the Play parameters in previous versions, Track parameters in Cubase SX cannot be applied to individual MIDI parts. Instead, they are always set up for complete MIDI tracks.

Drum Tracks

Unlike previous incarnations, there is no longer a specific track class for drums. Instead, you can assign a drum map to any MIDI track. This will give you the same drum-editing features as in previous Cubase versions.

Mixing

Mixing MIDI is now done in the Track Mixer, along with your audio channels. The MIDI channel strips are similar to the channel strips in the MIDI Track Mixer, allowing you to set levels, panning and other parameters for your MIDI tracks.

What's Completely New In Cubase SX?

At the risk of sounding repetitive, it can't be over-emphasised that Cubase SX is a completely rewritten application built on the foundations and technology of Steinberg's aristocratic Nuendo. As a bit of useless information, you might like to know that the SX tag was added to reinforce the complete rebirth of this application and, perhaps more prosaically, was named after Essex by its developers as the codename for the project, for some reason. (I suppose we should just be grateful that the development team had never heard of Scunthorpe!) Since SX is a completely new incarnation of Cubase, it's worth glancing through the list of totally new features before you get stuck into any serious production work. Powerful new features and functionality include:

Multiple Undo And Redo

Cubase SX offers an all-singing, all-dancing, wide-ranging multiple Undo facility which, as it says on the tin, allows you to undo virtually any action you perform.

Edit History

The Edit History dialog now allows you to undo or redo several actions in one go.

Offline Process History

The Offline Process History allows you to remove and modify applied processing. This is actually different from the 'regular' Undo function in that you don't have to undo processing functions in the order that they were performed.

Graphic Editing Of Automation Events

Automation handling has also been greatly improved in Cubase SX. Automation events can now be drawn graphically in the Project window, and each audio and MIDI track in the Track list has an automation track containing all parameters for each selected track. You can select which parameters to view and edit by opening subtracks for the automation track. You can also, of course, use normal Write and Read automation to record your actions, just as you could in previous versions of Cubase. On top of that, all effect control panels also feature Write and Read buttons and each automated effect and VST instrument has its own automation track in the Track list, with subtracks for each parameter.

Surround Sound

Cubase SX has introduced integrated surround-sound features with support for several popular formats.

Integration

The newly crafted graphic design in Cubase SX integrates all of the various windows in a much clearer way than in previous versions – for example, the Inspector, the Track list and the Track Mixer have many shared parameters which all use the same style of buttons, allowing you to alter a range of settings quickly and intuitively in whichever window you're currently working.

Hitpoints

Hitpoint editing is a new feature of the Sample Editor which allows you to create 'slices' of data to be used in drum loops, or indeed those of any instrument. A sliced loop can then adapt to changes in tempo without its pitch being affecting. The previous system of using tempo- and time-based hitpoints for matching time and metre positions, found in Cubase VST, is no longer used.

VST System Link

This is a new system for networking computers using VST software and ASIO (Audio Stream Input/Output) hardware allowing you to work with multiple computers (including cross-platform systems) and to dedicate certain tasks to different computers. For example, you could run all VST instruments on one computer, all audio tracks on another and so on.

Summary

Writing a book that explains every aspect of every feature in a program like Cubase SX would be a thankless and, to be quite honest, futile task. Since music doesn't consist of a single genre, the requirements of all musicians can't be generalised or anticipated in a single volume. As a practising musician or producer, the type or style of music that you wish to produce will ultimately dictate which features and functions and precisely how much of Cubase SX's power you will actually want or need to use. As it happens, I tend to consider myself a musician and composer first and a producer second, which is why this book – although hopefully as comprehensive as possible for a fast guide – is designed primarily to introduce practising musicians, in particular, to the skills and techniques required to use the essential elements of Cubase SX, whether they've read the manual or not. It's also designed specifically for musicians and producers who traditionally hate manuals and prefer a more heuristic approach, dipping into features and functionality as and when the need arises. Basically, the idea is to familiarise you with the essence of Cubase SX so that you're free to create the music you hear in your head but have, perhaps, been unable to realise in a recorded form...until now.

Cubase is such a mind-bogglingly massive application that, for the purposes of this book, I will assume that you have at least a familiarity with the inner workings of your PC and at least a reasonable familiarity with Cubase VST. I've also not gone into a lot of technical detail concerning add-on audio cards or peripherals, since these will vary considerably depending on your own personal studio set-up. However, when it comes to add-ons and MIDI devices, I can't recommend strongly enough that you actually read the manuals and documentation. Yes, it *is* boring, but in these instances it's the only hope you have of getting everything working together in a reasonably harmonious fashion.

If you're at all like me, you believe that music is magic, and ultimately the magic of music creation always depends on something totally indefinable, something that turns a riff, a break or a chord sequence into something transcendental. Sometimes it's hard work and good intentions, but sometimes it's serendipity or dumb luck. As it happens, a good digital-audio workstation running Cubase SX really can cater for nearly all of your creative-recording studio needs, but you still have to remember that it won't write your songs for you and it doesn't come with creativity and talent plug-ins. As clever and as powerful as this technology might be, it's worth reflecting on that notion As you'll see through reading this book, some level of technical involvement is inevitable, and you'll need to browse the manual and peripheral documentation that comes with the program, at least. And to get the most out of Cubase SX, you'll also have to consider things like microphones, monitors, effects, room acoustics, tuning and all the other stuff you'd usually have to think about in any other recording environment. That's why the real secret for musicians and producers alike is simply to know the limits of the software, however few they might be, and to be properly equipped before taking the musical plunge. Luckily, with Steinberg's Cubase SX, you have the freedom and ability to choose just how deeply you wish or, more importantly, need to go. When you're working with any digital equipment, it's worth reminding yourself on a regular basis that, just because you can, it doesn't mean you should. Sure, the user interface and level of functionality can always be adapted to each individual's personal needs and preferences, but somewhere along the line it's you, the musician, who needs to know how to enhance that power and add the essential element of magic.

1 FIRST STEPS

Although Cubase SX is available for both Mac and Windows, all the examples in this book are shown for the PC. In a bid for continuity, Steinberg has ensured that screens on both system look and work pretty much the same. However, if you are using a PC, be aware that you're going to require a pretty heavy-duty system running Windows 2000 or XP to handle the torque. Like it or not, Cubase SX is formally unsupported, if not totally, and probably completely incompatible with systems running Windows 9x, ME or NT. So, if you've got a PC running any of those earlier systems, stop reading now and go out and upgrade your kit. As well as an up-to-date version of Windows, you'll also need a PC with at least one USB port, which shouldn't pose too much of a problem these days. Steinberg maintain that, by not supporting 'legacy' systems, they've been able to provide a better product by focusing on newer technology to improve performance. However, for a lot of potential users, this does mean spending more money.

The minimum requirements for running Cubase SX are

a lot more strict than with previous versions, and you won't be able to get anywhere without at least a 500MHz Pentium III with a minimum of 256Mb of RAM. Since this sort of spec is fairly typical of more modern PCs sold with Windows XP, this also shouldn't pose much of a problem, unless you're still running vintage kit. You should also ensure that your display has a resolution of no less than 1,024 x 768. Certain windows in Cubase SX need at least this much space just to be fully visible, and of course two screens are always better than one, if you can afford them.

The main reason why you'll need a free USB port is because Steinberg, in its infinite wisdom, uses a dongle as a security device. With Cubase SX, this plugs into a USB port and replaces the previous parallel-port device which caused so many disruptive hassle for PC users when Cubase VST version 5 was first released.

I have to go on record at this point to say that I hate dongles and think they're a dreadfully intrusive method of copy protection which will always play havoc with your system in one way or another. In a word, they suck. As a Mac user, I never had to suffer the indignities of a dongle with Cubase VST 5, and it's my opinion that Steinberg could have come up with a better and less intrusive security option for the PC as well. OK, piracy is a problem, but the reality is that cracked versions of Cubase SX were available on the net when the application was still in its beta stages, and even before its general worldwide release cracked versions with dongle bypasses were also available. So why use a security mechanism that doesn't fully protect the application and yet has the potential to cause seriously annoying problems for legitimate users who have actually paid good money for the program? But, as I said, that's only my opinion.

Early comments from Steinberg suggested that this new dongle could also be used to store additional data for other product authorisation. So, for example, at some point in time you could find that you needed it to provide copy-protection information for all of your plug-in instruments and effects, which (again, depending on your point of view) could be seen as a blessing or a curse if and/or when it decides to pack up in the course of your recording or mixing. As a concession to customer loyalty, Steinberg has allowed users of Cubase VST version 5 to keep their original dongles when upgrading, and both applications generally seem to co-exist on the same machine. Oh yes, and you always have to remember that the dongle needs to be plugged into the computer's USB port after installing Cubase SX and restarting the computer.

If you plug it in first, you'll probably experience a few recognition problems. When the dongle is plugged into the USB port, Windows will automatically register it as a new hardware device and will attempt to find drivers for it. As you might expect, these necessary drivers won't be there until Cubase SX has been installed and the computer has been restarted.

Installing SX And Setting Up Your System

Before you do anything else, you should set up your specific audio hardware and its drivers. There are a lot of options available for soundcards, so suffice it to say that you'll need to install your chosen card and related equipment in your particular PC, following the card's instructions. Once you've done this, you'll need to install the particular driver specified for the card. There are three types of drivers that could apply: card-specific ASIO drivers, DirectX drivers and common Windows Multimedia drivers

ASIO Driver

If your soundcard has a specific ASIO driver, it will most likely be included with the card itself. However, you should always check the card manufacturer's website for the most recent drivers and updates. And I know that this can be a drag, but you'll need to refer to the manufacturer's instructions for details on how to install the driver.

DirectX Driver

If your audio card is DirectX compatible, its DirectX drivers will most likely be installed when you install the card, as is also the case with the ubiquitous Windows Multimedia driver. If you've downloaded special DirectX drivers for the audio card, you should once again follow the manufacturer's installation instructions.

Windows Multimedia Driver

This driver is fairly common and is normally included with all types of regular PC audio cards, and some such drivers are even included with Windows itself. The method of the audio card's installation depends on whether it's 'plug-and-play compatible'. If it is, Windows will detect the card once it's plugged in and will ask for the necessary driver disks. If not, you'll need to use the 'Add New Hardware' control panels to install the card and its drivers. And again, it might be boring, but you'll still have to refer to the documentation that comes with the card. If, for whatever reason, you find yourself with an audio card but no driver, be sure to check the manufacturer's website or ask your music or computer dealer for help.

To make sure that the audio card works as expected, you can run two simple tests. Firstly, use any software included with the audio card to make sure that you can record and play back audio without any problems. Secondly, if your card is accessed via a standard Windows driver, use the Media Player application included with Windows to play back an audio file. If this works, you know your card is installed properly.

Installing A MIDI Interface

In order to use MIDI, you'll need at least one MIDI interface, at least one MIDI instrument and some sort of audio equipment over which to listen to the sound generated by your gear. Although working with MIDI can appear somewhat arcane, installation instructions for a MIDI interface are normally included with the product, although you might find that a degree of trial and error and experimentation is necessary when installing devices. Generally, you'll need to install the interface or MIDI synthesiser card inside your computer or physically connect it to a port on your PC, depending on which type of interface you have. If your interface has a power supply and/or a power switch, turn it on – you should then be able to install the interface's driver as described in the accompanying documentation. It's likely that you'll need a CD-ROM or – shock, horror! – a floppy disk, which should be supplied by the manufacturer of the MIDI interface, and you'll probably have to play mix-and-match with your cable connections as well.

Hardware Requirements

PC

As mentioned briefly earlier on, the absolute minimum requirements for running Cubase SX on a PC include a 500MHz Pentium III processor with 256Mb of RAM or an equivalent AMD processor. Steinberg's recommended configuration for optimum performance includes a 1GHz or faster dual Pentium III/Athlon processor with 512Mb of RAM, and as always in this department, more is better.

RAM

If you've ever done any work with audio, you'll know that it requires literally shedloads of RAM. In fact, there is a direct correlation between the amount of available RAM and the number of audio channels that you can have running at any one time. Like I said, 256Mb is the minimum requirement, but again size does matter and bigger really is better, and this is true of RAM just as it is of storage.

Hard-Disk Size

The size of your hard disk determines how many minutes of audio you'll be able to record. Believe it or not, recording one minute of stereo-CD-quality audio requires around 10Mb of hard-disk space. This means that eight stereo tracks in Cubase SX use up at least 80Mb of disk space per recording minute. And while Cubase is still generally seen as being an excellent MIDI sequencer, I can vouch for its equally excellent audio capabilities. My last album, which consisted of only acoustic audio and vocal tracks, was produced and mastered entirely on Cubase and still retains a warm, well-rounded, mellow sound.

It's also worth pointing out that the speed of your hard drive also determines the number of audio tracks that you can run at once. Known as *sustained transfer rate*, the quantity of information that the disk can read is reliant on the speed of your drive – and once again, more is good, while a lot more is even better.

Wheel Mouse

While a normal, run-of-the-mill mouse will work perfectly well with Cubase SX, Steinberg recommend the use of a wheel mouse, as they're convinced that this will considerably speed up value-editing and scrolling. Since I didn't have access to a wheel mouse when writing this book, I'll just have to take their word for it. However, like everything else to do with Cubase SX, your own personal working practices and musical requirements will determine the minutiae of how you set up your system.

Installing Cubase SX

Installing Cubase SX is a pleasantly painless exercise. All you have to do is insert the CD-ROM, follow the prompts that appear onscreen, plug in your dongle and, as they say, Bob's your uncle – and since I actually have an Uncle Bob, the whole process was even easier! If, as is generally the case these days, you're connected to the internet, the installation program will even contact Steinberg to check on any available updates, patches and fixes and give you the option of downloading and installing them. (It's also worth running this utility from time to time after installation to ensure that you've got the latest version of the software and any necessary fixes.) As I mentioned earlier, it's important that you remember to plug in the dongle after you've completed the installation procedure and you've restarted your computer. After you've done this, when you open the Windows Start menu, you'll find a Cubase SX group in the Programs submenu containing the following items.

ASIO DirectX Full Duplex Set-up

This is the dialog box where you can choose your settings if your audio hardware uses DirectX drivers for audio playback and recording.

ASIO Multimedia Set-up

This opens a dialog box in which you can choose settings for your ASIO system, which, if you're using the ASIO MME driver, handles audio recording and playback in Cubase SX. You can also open this dialog from within Cubase SX itself.

Cubase SX

This command does exactly what it says on the tin and, as you might expect, launches the actual program. You might also notice some additional items present here such as 'Read Me' files available on the Start menu. Even if you hate manuals, it's probably a good idea to read these files before you go about launching Cubase SX, as they might contain additional information not included in the manuals.

LCC

This item shows all SyncroSoft protection devices and the usual boring valid licences currently installed.

A Word On Soundcards

When it comes to soundcards, Steinberg recommends the use of any audio hardware that supports the ASIO protocol in order to ensure low latency values and trouble-free operation. Since most soundcard manufacturers have adapted to this standard and provide drivers for all of the latest operating systems, finding a suitable soundcard for your particular system shouldn't be difficult. Generally speaking, unless you try to run SX on an under-powered machine and a crappy Soundblaster-style soundcard, you won't encounter any major problems. It's also worth pointing out that Cubase SX doesn't provide any input-level adjustment for audio, since this is performed differently for each card. Adjusting input levels is done either in a special application included with the hardware or possibly from its ASIO control panel.

Studio Configurations

There are a variety of ways of configuring your studio set-up, depending on your requirements and preferences, the style of music you're producing and your production and individual working practices. Since I work primarily on a Mac, I was able to create this book with the help of Piotr (e-manuel) Dorosz, who engineered and co-produced my last album, which was recorded in part at Tonic Studios in Hastings. Obviously, the hardware configuration for the studio might be somewhat posher than the average home system, but it does give you an idea of the sort of power you'll need if you really want to push Cubase SX to the limits. The newest custom-built computer set-up that we used to evaluate Cubase SX essentially consisted of the following:

- Radeon 9700 Atlantis Pro (ATI Radeon 9700 Pro chipset, 128Mb DDR, 325/310, DVI, TVO)

- Intel Pentium 4 2.53GHz (533MHz) Northwood processor, 512k cache

- Thermaltake A1358 18" ATA133 round cable

- Maxtor 6Yo8oLo DiamondMax Plus9 80GB UDMA133 (for audio)

- IBM 120GB UDMA 100 (for OS)

- Pioneer DVD-106S

- Crucial 512Mb 184-pin DIMM PC2100 DDR RAM, non-parity CL2.5 (times three = 1.5Gb RAM)

- Abit BD7-II-RAID motherboard

- Yamaha CRW-F1E-VK

- Windows 2000 Professional

- Cubase SX 1.03

- Hammerfall RME HDSP Multiface with PCI card

Basic Cubase SX

- ADSL 512kbs

- Networked 100 Fast Ethernet with three other PCs

- Two 19" flat-panel TFT iiyama monitors

- Creative Labs Soundblaster Live! (for system sounds and SoundFont playback)

- Quiet aluminium PC case, power-supply unit and removable hard-drive enclosure

In view of the above, sticking to Steinberg's minimum specs will still provide you with an excellent recording and production environment. However, aspiration is good, I'm told, and obviously the more powerful system you can afford to use, the more power you can wrench from Cubase SX.

2 GETTING STARTED

Like all modern sequencers, Cubase SX uses a sophisticated graphic interface that allows blocks of sound or MIDI information to be copied, sliced and moved around, while audio and MIDI recordings are visible within the same window to make editing and tracking easier by showing you exactly where your audio sources are in relation to your MIDI data. With the addition of VST (Virtual Studio Technology), Cubase and a few add-ons can easily cater for nearly all of your recording and production needs. OK, if you're a fanatical audio purist or an anal-retentive techie geek, you'll always be able to find something that's not absolutely perfect with various recordings, whether they're done on a PC at home or in a commercial studio, but as the *I Ching* says, perseverance furthers, and if you know your music and know the sound you want, Cubase SX is more than capable of helping you achieve that special blend you're after.

Before you can get down to some serious recording, however, you'll need to be able to find your way around the various windows and controls in Cubase SX. The main windows provide access to various tools and key-control elements that will enable you to unlock the full power and functionality of Cubase SX. However, like driving a strange car or learning to fly an F-16, knowing where all the controls are and understanding exactly what they do can be a definite advantage.

The Transport Panel

In Cubase SX, the Transport panel, like the familiar, traditional buttons found on analogue tape or video players, is used for controlling Record/Playback and other transport functions. With these controls you can play your recording, stop, wind forward or rewind just as you can on an analogue system. However, in Cubase SX, the Transport panel offers additional functionality and control over things like tempo and time signatures. It's also worth noting that the main transport functions – Play, Stop, Cycle and Record – are also available.

Left and right locator display, used to define where to start and end recording and which section to cycle

Position display

Tempo and time signature display

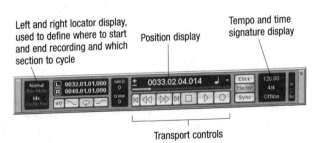

Transport controls

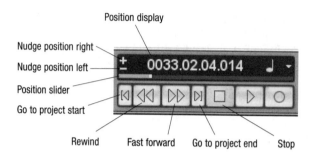

Position display

Nudge position right

Nudge position left

Position slider

Go to project start

Rewind   Fast forward   Go to project end   Stop

0033.02.04.014

At the far left of the Transport panel, you'll see the Record Mode selector. This determines whether Cubase SX will add any existing sound when recording takes place or overwrite what you've already recorded. The Record Mode selector affects only MIDI data and won't alter your audio recordings.

Immediately to the right of the Record Mode selector is a panel that contains settings for the left and right locators, the Cycle buttons, buttons for punching in and out of recordings and the AutoQuantize button. As you might guess, the top box indicates the current positions of the locators and defines where to start and end recording or what section to cycle. If you click on one of the locator labels (left or right), your song position is moved to the corresponding locator.

The Cycle button is used for cycling between the left and right locator positions. A cycle is essentially nothing more than a loop, the start and end points of which can be determined by setting the positions of the left and right locators. When the Cycle function is activated, you can listen to a section of your arrangement over and over again, recording more information each time.

If you've used a Portastudio or similar multitrack recorder or have done any work in a traditional studio you'll be familiar with a technique called *punching in*, or *dropping in*. This is the process of recording a new bit of a song onto a track while the tape is rolling. This function is particularly useful if you mess up a section of a vocal or lead line but the rest of the recording is actually OK. You simply run back the recording and drop in a replacement section over the flawed section and either punch out or carry on until the end. You can use either an automatic or a manual punch in.

TIP

If you've got a vocal or instrumental bit that's slightly off pitch and it's only a small section of an otherwise acceptable performance, don't drop or punch in a replacement. Instead, try using a pitch-correction plug-in to tweak and match the offending slips. With vocals, particularly, this maintains the feeling and organic flow of a piece, which can often be lost with a drop-in.

With the AutoQuantize button, you can choose to quantize everything you record, according to whatever quantizing type you've selected. As with practically everything in Cubase SX, if the result isn't what you expected or intended, it can easily be undone. (Incidentally, automatic quantizing applies only to MIDI recording and not to audio.)

Above these controls are two timing-display bars, one showing the current song position in bars, beats and ticks and one a time-code readout showing the current song position in hours, minutes, seconds and frames.

At the far right, you'll find controls for activating the metronome, tempo and time-signature readouts and indicators that show MIDI-in (recording) and -out (playback) activity. There's also a Sync button for synchronising the sequencer to external devices. As you're probably aware, tempo determines the actual speed of your music and the number of beats per minute (usually quarter notes) and the time signature – ie 4/4, 3/4, etc – determines the overall feel of the beat and the grouping of notes. Perhaps the easiest way to set the tempo is to activate playback and adjust the tempo on the

Transport panel while listening to the metronome pulse (triggered by the Click button) generated on each beat.

If necessary, you can change the size of the Transport panel and decide which parts of it you wish to be visible at any time. If you right-click anywhere within the Transport panel, a pop-up menu will appear from which you can check or uncheck elements of the Transport panel as desired.

The Project Window

This is the main window in Cubase SX and provides you with an accessible graphic overview of your project, allowing you to navigate and get down to some hardcore editing. This is the magic circle (or, in this case, rectangle) in which you actually record and assemble your songs. Cubase was the first sequencer to implement the now-ubiquitous graphic Arrange window, allowing musical sections to be represented as rectangular blocks along a timeline. In Cubase SX, the Project window replaces the traditional Arrange window and song files have been superseded by project files, now identified with the .cpr extension.

Essentially, the Project window is divided vertically into tracks and has a timeline running horizontally from left to right. Each project has one Project window. Unlike previous versions of Cubase, such as VST, where you could have several Arrange windows, Cubase SX allows you to have only one Project window open at once. However, with SX you can have several projects open simultaneously, whereas with VST you could have only

The Cubase SX Project window

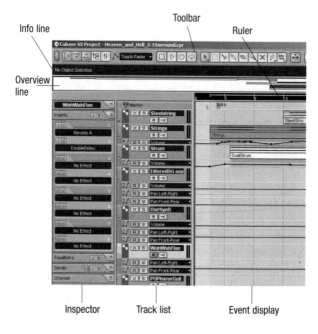

Toolbar

Info line

Ruler

Overview line

Inspector

Track list

Event display

41

one song open at a time. It's also now possible for several projects to share the same Project folder. In SX, each audio track in the Project window is now automatically assigned to a unique audio channel, which unfortunately makes it impossible for multiple audio tracks to share the same channel, as they could before. Critics have complained that multiple takes of the same part now each require a separate audio channel when they're essentially part of the same track. However, in some respects, this new structure does force you to adopt a more organised way of working.

The new Project window does provide significantly more editing capabilities than previous versions of Cubase did, and it's now possible to edit with single-sample accuracy. Audio events can be displayed directly in the Project window, and all of the audio that you record or import into an SX project will always start off as an audio event. (In previous versions, the Arrange window could display only parts or collections of audio events, and it's still possible to make a collection of audio events into a part, which can be edited in the Audio Editor, as before. This can be particularly useful when you want to compile multiple vocal takes.) In SX, audio events are displayed with 'handles' that allow you to adjust the start and end points easily. You can also add fade-ins and fade-outs and adjust the overall level relative to the audio channel playing a particular audio event.

Track Types

In Cubase SX, you have the following track types are available in the Project window:

Audio

As you would imagine, you can use this track for recording and playing back audio events and parts. Each audio track has a corresponding audio channel in the Mixer, and an audio track can have any number of automation 'subtracks' for doing clever things like automating mixer-channel parameters and inserting effect settings.

Folder

As with folders on your PC, folder tracks here function as containers for other tracks, allowing you to edit several tracks at the same time, among other things.

Group Channels

Group channels function as subgroups and allow you to route several audio channels to a dedicated group channel. Afterwards, you can mix them with a single set of controls, allowing you to do things like apply the same effects to them. A group-channel track contains no events as such but displays settings and automation curves for the corresponding group channel, and each has a corresponding channel strip in the Mixer.

MIDI Tracks

These are what you use for recording and playing back MIDI parts, and each MIDI track also has a corresponding MIDI channel strip in the Mixer. You can assign a MIDI track to have a number of automation 'subtracks' to enable the automating of parameters of Mixer channels, insert and send effect settings, etc.

Marker Track

The marker track displays...yes, you guessed it, markers, which can be moved and renamed in the Project window. There can be only one marker track in each project.

Master Automation

This control contains automation curves for master volume and global effect input levels, and, like the marker track, there can only be one Master Automation track in each project. However, you can expand the Master Automation control to display any number of curves.

Plug-in Automation

In SX, each send effect, master effect or VST instrument can have its own individual plug-in automation track, allowing for automation of all plug-in parameters. A plug-in automation track is automatically created the first time you automate any of a plug-in's parameters.

Video Tracks

I won't say too much about these, but they're for playing back video events. If you do need to use this, remember that a project can have only one video track.

Parts And Events

Think of events as Lego-like building blocks. When you build your project, you'll find that different event types are handled differently in the Project window, as follows:

- Video events and automation events (curve points) are viewed and rearranged in the Project window.

- MIDI events are always gathered in MIDI parts, while containers for one or more MIDI events and MIDI parts are rearranged and manipulated in the Project window. To edit the individual MIDI events in a part, you have to open the part in a MIDI editor.

- Audio events can be displayed and edited directly in the Project window, but you can also work with audio parts containing several events. This is particularly useful if you have a number of events that you want to treat as one unit in the project.

An audio event (left) and an audio part (right)

The Track List

On the left in the Project window you'll find the Track list, which contains name fields and various settings for each track. Different track types have different controls in the Track list. Depending on your display size, to see all of the controls you might have to experiment with resizing the required track in the Track list.

The Inspector

Moving unfashionably further to the left, you'll find an area called the Inspector. This can show additional controls and parameters for the track selected in the Track list, and if several are selected, it shows the setting for the first (topmost) selected track. To hide or show the Inspector, click the Inspector icon in the toolbar.

The contents and usage of the Inspector depends on the selected track's class. For some classes of track, the Inspector is divided into sections. You can hide or show sections by clicking the tabs in their top-

Track list areas for audio tracks. The top image shows the default view while the bottom image shows the expanded setting

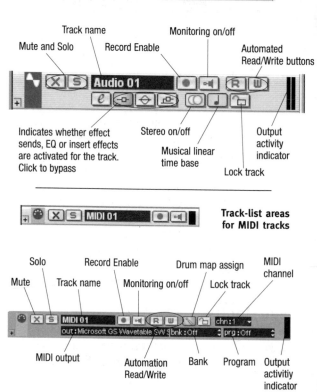

Track name

Monitoring on/off

Mute and Solo

Record Enable

Automated Read/Write buttons

Audio 01

Indicates whether effect sends, EQ or insert effects are activated for the track. Click to bypass

Stereo on/off

Musical linear time base

Lock track

Output activity indicator

Track-list areas for MIDI tracks

Solo

Record Enable

Drum map assign

MIDI channel

Mute

Track name

Monitoring on/off

Lock track

MIDI 01

out : Microsoft GS Wavetable SW S bnk : Off   prg : Off   chn : 1

MIDI output

Automation Read/Write

Bank

Program

Output activitiy indicator

Basic Cubase SX

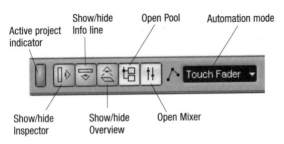

Active project indicator

Show/hide Info line

Open Pool

Automation mode

Show/hide Inspector

Show/hide Overview

Open Mixer

Touch Fader

The Cubase SX inspector

right-hand corners. Clicking the tab for a hidden section brings it into view and hides the other sections, while [Ctrl]-clicking the tab allows you to hide or show a section without affecting other sections. Finally, Alt-clicking a tab shows or hides all sections in the Inspector. (It should be noted that folding a section does not affect the functionality but merely hides the section from view. In other words, if you've set up a track parameter or activated an effect, your settings will still be active even if you fold the Inspector section.)

The Toolbar

As in recent versions of Cubase, in SX, various tools used in different situations are gathered in toolboxes or toolbars. Most windows in Cubase SX have their own particular toolbar, each with appropriate variations. Essentially, the toolbar contains tools and shortcuts for opening other windows and various project settings and functions.

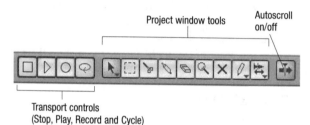

Project window tools

Autoscroll on/off

Transport controls
(Stop, Play, Record and Cycle)

The Cubase SX Toolbar

In some respects, the toolbox familiar in earlier versions of Cubase has been superseded in SX. The Quick menu is displayed as a normal Windows pop-up menu, although it still provides a selection of tools to which users have become accustomed. In SX, the Quick menu also provides a list of context-sensitive options based on whichever elements you've currently selected onscreen and the position of the mouse when you clicked to access the menu.

The toolbox is now also displayed along the toolbar of every window, providing a second method of accessing whatever you need for editing. SX will now let you select tools via the number keys on the main PC keyboard – not, as you might think, from the numeric keypad. Logically, the keys that select the various tools – number keys 1-8 – follow the same running order as the tools that normally appear in the Project window. However, in a most un-Spock-like illogical manner, in other editors where the order of the tools differs, the number keys still dumbly follow the order in the Project window.

The Info Line

The Info line shows information about whichever event or part has been selected in the Project window. You can edit almost all values in the Info line by using regular value editing. Length and position values are displayed in the format currently selected for the ruler, and the Info line can be hidden or revealed by clicking the corresponding icon on the toolbar. The following elements can also be selected for display and editing on the Info line:

- Audio events
- Audio parts
- MIDI parts
- Video events
- Markers
- Automation-curve points

The Cubase SX Info line

It's worth noting that the Info line will display information only if a single element is selected.

The Ruler

This is found at the top of the Event display and shows the Timeline. Initially, the Ruler in the Project window uses the display format specified in the Project Setup dialog box, just like all of the other rulers and position displays in the project. However, you can select an independent display format for the Ruler by clicking on the arrow button to the right of it and selecting an option from the pop-up menu that appears. The selection you make here affects the Ruler, the Info line and tool-tip position values appearing when you drag an event in the Project window. You can also select independent formats for other rulers and position displays. To set the display format globally for all windows, use the Display Format pop-up menu on the Transport panel or hold down [Ctrl] and select a display format in any ruler.

The Project window Ruler

Cubase SX – Short Back And Sides

Cubase SX is one of those applications that can stretch as far as you want to stretch it. As I said in the introduction, this book is designed particularly for musicians and producers who simply want to have a go at creating music with a digital studio. Sure, hardcore tech-heads or even sound engineers and technicians with loads of traditional studio experience will be able to use Cubase SX and explain everything you never wanted to know about decibels, waveforms, impedance, ohms, room acoustics and the like, and it's cool and extremely impressive that an application like Cubase SX can offer so much to so many different users. But don't be overawed by all the science and, above all, don't let it get in the way of the music. As long as you've got a reasonably good microphone, some basic MIDI kit and perhaps some sort of sampling capability, you can easily produce music that will sound as good, if not better, than most of the stuff currently being produced commercially. OK, maybe that's not all that hard and should probably be discouraged at all costs. However, if you want to know all the related science and techie bits, there are plenty of books out there to choose from. If you just want to play, compose and record interesting music, then learn how to do what you need for what you want to produce, even if you don't fully comprehend all the jargon and technical explanations behind it.

Science or no science, though, before you get down to some serious recording, you do have to have some idea of how to get an audio signal into your PC, how to record and manipulate MIDI data and how you're then going to produce it in a form that you can feed back into the real world.

What Is Digital Audio?

Audio, or just plain sound, comes from any source that you can connect to a sound input on your PC. With the right bits and pieces, you can use a microphone, keyboard, electric guitar – essentially, anything with a plug. Raw audio input becomes digital audio when your PC and add-on soundcard converts the signal into numbers (via an analogue-to-digital converter) which Cubase SX then captures and stores on your hard drive. Once your digital audio is in the box, you can creatively start to manipulate and process your recordings. As I mentioned earlier, it's absolutely vital to remember that audio files tend to be exceedingly large when they're written to your hard disk during the actual recording process. This is why storage size is important when it comes to planning your system, and also why you should always defragment your drive before starting a recording session.

The quality of your digital audio data depends entirely on the performance of the converters found in your audio card, as well as the data's sampling rate and bit resolution. When people talk about a sampling rate, all they mean is the number of times an analogue signal is measured each second, while bit resolution – usually found in measures of 8, 16, 20 and 24 – describes the accuracy of the system measuring the signal. The higher the number of bits, the more levels of resolution are available to measure the analogue signal. Assuming that your PC is meaty enough, each project in Cubase SX will support a maximum of 200 audio and 64 group tracks, with 96kHz sampling rates and up to 32-bit resolution. While every audio file in a project must use the same sample rate in Cubase SX, it's still possible to mix and match bit depths, if necessary. This can be particularly useful if you want to, say, bounce 16-bit audio tracks and keep the internal 32-bit resolution used by most insert effects.

Considering that bog-standard audio CDs handle only 16 bits, this high degree of resolution might seem like overkill, but in reality the situation is sort of analogous to graphics scanning: images are typically scanned at very high resolutions – up to 2,400 dots per square inch – even though no printing device on Earth can cope with such dense grids of ink. (Colour images are normally printed at a maximum of 200dpi, while greyscale ones seldom exceed 300dpi.) The reason for this is that the graphics expert gets far better results by scanning an image at these enormously high resolutions and then, when the image is ready for printing, 'dithering' down to a grid more acceptable to image setters and high-resolution laser printers. All the data is present in the original file and can be reprocessed, if necessary. Audio can be treated in exactly the same way, although in the end all CD-based audio must be reduced to 16 bits, as far greater initial accuracy can be obtained by scanning (ie recording) at these very high resolutions and then mastering at 16 bits.

If you've ever worked with Portastudios or some other kind of analogue multitrack recorder, you should understand that there are some aspects of working with digital audio that require a different approach. In traditional studios, it's not unusual to push certain sound signals so that VU meters occasionally peak into the red. In an analogue environment, this sort of technique can add a natural kind of warmth to a mix, and although it produces mild, graduated distortion, this tends to be rounded off and is hardly ever offensive to the ear. With digital audio, however, you can't allow levels to go into the red without getting a truly nasty distortion known as *clipping*. With Cubase SX, you must therefore ensure that no clipping occurs, and you might find that you need to record at analogue sources lower average levels than you're used to.

However, as I suggested earlier, you'll find that the advantages offered by digital audio generally outweigh the occasional disadvantages. Apart from the convenience of storing it on your hard disk, digital audio tends to have less background noise and hiss, provides a better dynamic range and can be copied with no loss of quality. And with Cubase SX and an assortment of VST plug-ins, you can easily apply a whole range of signal-processing effects.

What Is MIDI?

MIDI is another one of those annoying acronyms and stands for Musical Instrument Digital Interface. It's essentially a form of computer code that was developed as a means by which synths and other devices could be connected up so that they could talk to and interact with one another. For any techies that may have tuned in, MIDI is an asynchronous, serial interface transmitted at the rate of 31.25kbaud, or 31,250 bits per second. For the rest of us, a MIDI synthesiser or similar device works a bit like a musical printer – your PC sends information to it specifying the notes, sound, instrument type etc that you want to play and it gets on with creating the actual audio. This means that you can take a recording made on, say, a piano and play it back on a guitar sound just by changing the settings on your synth.

General MIDI, or GM as it's usually referred to, was an attempt to create a standard system for MIDI parameters whereby songs created on one GM-compatible synth could be played back on any other GM synth and sound something like the original. In other words, if an original composition specifies particular sounds to be played, then when any other GM synth is handed the GM MIDI file to play it will reproduce the correct sounds assigned by the original composer.

However, GM does have two main restrictions. One is that you're tied to a fairly standard, unadventurous palette of sounds, so if you've created some wicked tune featuring a clever little sound that you've programmed on some non-GM device, this sound won't be recognised by GM and could come out sounding like a duck.

The other restriction involves controllers. Since GM specifies fixed controller numbers for certain functions, while basic parameters such as pan, volume and sustain are represented, unfortunately more advanced functions such as filter resonance and cut-off time are not.

GM was agreed as a standard in 1991 by the JMSC (Japanese MIDI Standards Committee) and the MMA (American MIDI Manufacturers' Association). General MIDI System Level 1 specifies 24-note polyphonic, 16-part multitimbral operation; all of the drum sounds are defined by note number and the 128 sound patches for the other instruments are also defined.

GS And XG

There are also extensions of the GM standard called GS and XG. GS is Roland's extended version of GM which adds some extras on top of the GM settings by utilising the GM Bank Select command. MIDI has a fixed range of 0–127 for all parameters (although some manufacturers use 1–128), so original GM allows for only 128 sound patches, all stored in one bank, while the GM Bank Select command allows for further banks to be accessed, each with a further 128 patches. Also added are extra NRPNs (Non-Registered Parameter Numbers), which provide extra controller numbers, allowing you to twiddle things like filter control and envelope control and giving you extra effects parameters. In practice, GS files will play back on a GM synth, but none of the extras will be recognised by anything other than another GS-compatible device.

As with the Roland GS standard, XG is Yamaha's own dedicated version, also offering extra sounds and control parameters. However, these are not recognisable by GM or Roland, and vice versa.

Parts And Events

When you're recording MIDI or entering MIDI data manually in an editor, you're creating *MIDI events*. Each note you record is a separate MIDI event, for example, and if you record the movement of a modulation wheel or other controller, a large number of densely spaced MIDI events are created. MIDI events are always grouped in *MIDI parts*, which can be thought of as containers, allowing you to move or copy a number of MIDI events as one item. These MIDI parts are placed on MIDI tracks, and for each MIDI track you can specify on which MIDI output and MIDI channel its MIDI events should be played back. This allows you to have different tracks playing back different sounds on the same or different MIDI instruments.

OK, while MIDI can seem a bit confusing and, indeed,

downright cantankerous to wire up properly, it's extremely useful when it comes to digital recording. However, you'll be pleased to know that Cubase SX supports not only General MIDI but also both extensions from Roland and Yamaha.

3 AUDIO AND MIDI

The way in which you configure your system for Cubase SX will ultimately depend on what kind of music you intend to make, what kind of external devices you require and how elaborate you want to make your personal recording environment. Obviously, for making even the simplest MIDI-based recordings, you'll need some sort of input device such as a synth, a MIDI keyboard and, perhaps, a sampler, while for audio recordings the minimum is probably a microphone of some description that will plug into the audio input of your PC or audio card or perhaps an electric guitar or bass. You might want to start with a small-scale system that provides the minimum set-up necessary to record and play MIDI and audio in Cubase and then work up to a larger set-up, or you might want to customise your own personalised system to look something like the digital-studio layouts suggested in the illustrations here. The audio connections shown over the page can be either digital or analogue, it doesn't really matter.

Setting Up Audio
Stereo Input And Output – The Simplest Connection

If you use only a stereo input and output from Cubase SX, you might connect your audio hardware directly to the input source – a mixer, for example – and the outputs to a power amplifier and speaker. When connecting an input source – a mixer, say – to your audio hardware, you should use an output bus or similar that's separate from the mixer's master output in order to avoid recording what you're playing back.

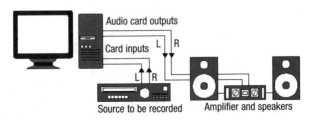

Stereo input/output set-up

Multichannel Input And Output

More often than not, you'll have other audio equipment that you want to integrate with Cubase SX. This will require a mixer, preferably one with a group or bus system that can be used for feeding inputs on the audio hardware. For example, you could use four buses for feeding signals to the sound hardware's inputs. Four outputs would be connected back to the mixer for monitoring and playback purposes and the remaining mixer inputs could then be used for connecting audio sources such as microphones, instruments and samplers.

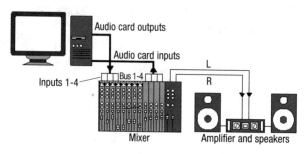

Multi-channel input/output set-up

Connecting For Surround Sound

If you plan to mix for surround sound, you could connect the audio outputs of your devices to a multichannel power amplifier driving a set of surround channels. For example, the connection shown over the page will work for mixing both 5.1 and LRCS (eg Pro Logic) where, say, two surround speakers will be playing the same material from a single surround channel. The only difference between the two formats here is the LFE channel, which isn't used with LRCS. Fortunately, Cubase SX supports a number of surround formats.

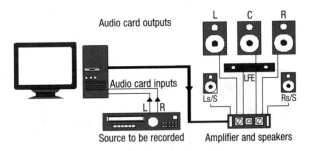

Surround-sound set-up

Recording From A CD Player

Most computers come equipped with a CD-ROM drive that can also be used as a regular CD player. Normally, the CD player is connected internally to the audio hardware so that you can record its output directly into Cubase SX. All routing and level adjustments are then done in the audio-hardware set-up application, shown in the illustration on page 67. It's also possible grab audio tracks directly from a CD and import them into Cubase SX.

Word Clock Connections

If you're using a digital audio connection, you might also need a Word Clock connection between the audio hardware and any external devices you're using. Don't forget that it's very important that you synchronise with the Word Clock correctly or you could end up with a lot of crackles and clicks on some of your recordings.

Audio Hardware Set-up

You'll often find that audio hardware has several inputs – say, for a microphone input, line inputs, assorted digital inputs and usually a connection from the CD-ROM drive in your PC. With audio hardware, you should receive one or more small applications that allow you to configure the inputs of the hardware to your own particular tastes. These sort of functions include:

- Selecting which in/outs are active

- Setting up Word Clock synchronisation (if available)

- Turning monitoring via hardware on/off

- Setting levels for each input

- Setting levels for the outputs so that they match the monitoring equipment you're using.

Basic Cubase SX

For more details about your audio-hardware set-up application, always refer to the documentation that came with the hardware. Yes, it is boring, but it's still important.

As I mentioned earlier on, Steinberg strongly recommend that you access your hardware via an ASIO driver written specifically for the hardware you're using, if available. If no ASIO driver is installed, they suggest that you check with the manufacturer of your audio hardware to see if they have an ASIO driver available – for download via the internet, for example. If your hardware doesn't have a specific ASIO driver, Steinberg state that a DirectX driver is the next best option.

To set up your own system, select 'Device Setup' from the Devices menu and click on 'VST Multitrack' in the list that pops up. Select your particular audio hardware from the ASIO Driver menu.

Click the Control Panel button and adjust the settings as recommended by the manufacturer of your audio hardware. Remember, the control panel that appears when you click on this button will be provided by the audio hardware manufacturer and not Cubase SX (unless you're using DirectX or MME), so settings will be different for each brand and model of audio card and may include options for such criteria as buffering,

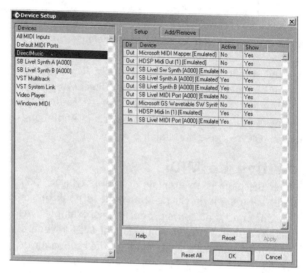

Device Setup menu

synchronisation and digital-input and -output formats. If you're planning to use several different audio applications simultaneously, you might want to activate the option 'Release ASIO Driver In Background', which will allow another application to play back via your audio hardware even when Cubase SX is running. In this instance, the application that is currently active, or sitting in the top window on the desktop, will get access to the audio hardware. Just make sure that any other audio applications accessing the audio hardware are also set to release the ASIO driver so that Cubase can use it when it becomes the active application again. (Incidentally, if your audio hardware and its driver support ASIO Direct Monitoring, you might want to activate the 'Direct Monitoring' checkbox.) When you've finished, click 'Apply' and then 'OK' to close the dialog box.

Setting Up MIDI

Over the page is an example of a fairly typical small MIDI set-up. You might need or want to hook things up differently, of course, and in this example I've assumed that you have some sort of MIDI keyboard and an external MIDI sound module. The keyboard can be used for feeding MIDI messages to your PC to activate the recording and playback of MIDI tracks, while the sound module is used for playback only. By using Cubase SX's MIDI Thru feature, you'll be able to hear the correct sound from the sound module while you're actually playing the keyboard or recording.

Of course, you might want to use even more instruments for playback, and if so, simply connect the MIDI Thru socket on the sound module to MIDI In of the next instrument, and so on. In this hook-up, you'll always play the first keyboard when recording, but you can still use all of your devices for providing sounds on playback. If you plan to use more than three sound sources, Steinberg recommend that you use either an interface with more than one output or a separate MIDI Thru box instead of the Thru jacks on each unit.

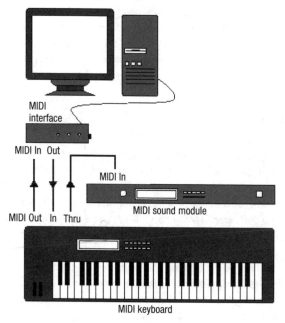

Typical MIDI set-up

Setting Up A Default MIDI Input And Output

You might want to make sure that any new tracks you create are set to particular MIDI ports, and fortunately this is fairly easy to do. To begin with, select 'Device Setup' from the Devices menu and click on 'Default MIDI Ports' in the list that appears. Make sure that the Setup tab is selected and then use the two pop-ups to select an input and an output. Now, newly created tracks will always use this input and output. (Don't worry – like most things in SX, you can change this setting for each individual track in the Project window at any time.) To finish off, click on 'Apply' and then 'OK' to close the dialog box.

TIP

You'll notice in Cubase SX that MIDI inputs and outputs can often be shown with unnecessarily long and complex names. However, if you like, you can rename your MIDI ports with shorter, sexier and more descriptive names. Simply open the 'Device Setup' dialog box from the Devices menu and select the Windows MIDI device in the Device list. The available MIDI inputs and outputs are all listed under the Setup tab. To change the name of a MIDI port, click in the Device column and type in a new name of the port. After closing the dialog box, the new name will appear on the MIDI In and Out windows, as well as in the pop-ups in the Inspector and Track Mixer.

Setting MIDI Thru And Local On/Off

To do this, first go to the File menu and open the Preferences dialog. In the MIDI section, you'll find a setting called 'MIDI Thru Active' which can be switched on or off. Its status is related to a setting in your instrument called 'Local On/Off' or 'Local Control On/Off'. MIDI Thru should be activated and instruments should be set to 'Local Off', or 'Local Control Off'. The MIDI signal from the keyboard will then be recorded into Cubase SX and at the same time rerouted back to the instrument so that you can hear what you're playing without having the keyboard triggering its own sounds.

If you're using a separate MIDI keyboard that doesn't produce any of its own sounds, MIDI Thru in Cubase SX should also be activated. This time you don't have to look for any Local On/Off settings in your instruments; the only occasion when MIDI Thru should be *deactivated* is when you're using Cubase SX with only one keyboard instrument and when that instrument can't be set to Local Off mode. You should also remember that MIDI Thru will only be active for MIDI tracks that are record enabled.

When MIDI Thru is active in Cubase SX, MIDI data received is immediately 'echoed' back out so that, when you press a key, it's sent out via MIDI to Cubase. Any MIDI data coming in to the instrument is then played by the synth inside it, so when Local (Control) is set to 'On' on the instrument, the keys you press will be played by the internal synth. When Local (Control) is set to Off, this connection is broken.

TIP

If you want to use remote-control devices, such as Steinberg's Houston, in conjunction with Cubase SX, it's important to observe that remote-control data is recorded to MIDI tracks and 'thrued' when the track input is set to 'All MIDI Inputs'. In some cases, not only the track mixer but also MIDI instruments routed to that track will be unintentionally remote-controlled. In order to avoid this, you should exclude single MIDI In ports from the 'All MIDI Input' setting. To do this, go to the Devices menu and open 'Device Setup'. There, in the category 'All MIDI Inputs', you'll see that individual MIDI In ports can be deactivated. From here, every MIDI in port that's accessed by a remote-control device should be deactivated.

Working Practices

Once you understand the basics of how Cubase SX works, the best way to master it is to get in there and start experimenting. Trial and error is an excellent teacher, and finding things out for yourself is always more valuable then being spoonfed someone else's opinions every step of the way. After all, that's the only way you'll ever develop your own unique approach and creative method. But before we look at some actual studio and recording tips, let's look at some of the other peripheral equipment you'll need to get the best results from Cubase SX and, indeed, your own performance.

Once your PC, MIDI and Cubase connections are sorted out, there are a few additional priorities that you really can't afford to neglect if you're interested in making serious recordings. Firstly, if your budget's tight and you have to cut corners, whatever you do, *don't* skimp on your microphones. This is one bit of advice that cannot be over-emphasised. I mean, think about it – despite all the clever digital trickery, it's still difficult to make the final sound you ultimately produce better than the original source signal. If your budget is limited, buy one or two high-quality mics rather than several low-quality ones. As a matter of fact, to begin with, if money is tight, buy only one exceptionally good mic; you can do more with one good mic than any number of substandard models, even though in some instances it might seem like having several cheaper ones would make sessions more convenient.

Effects And Processors

With the wide range of VST plug-ins available today, you don't need a massive rack full of signal processors – reverbs, delays, etc – to make a pro-quality recording; that sort of stuff always looks impressive, but when you come right down to it, it's not essential. If you can afford them, one or two good reverbs and a couple of good-quality compressors could be useful, and there are several decent low-priced reverbs currently on the market.

While there are advantages to some of these hardware processors, you should definitely check out the range of VST plug-ins that offer digital equivalents of all of these sorts of effects. OK, none of the hardware units I've mentioned is going to startle the world or give you a Top Ten hit, but if they're used correctly and creatively they can yield surprisingly professional results without sending you to the bank for a second mortgage.

Media Matters

Since the chances are you'll be recording directly to your hard drive, you won't have to worry too much about things like ADATs or multitrack tape. However, a DAT or MiniDisc recorder can be useful for dubbing down master mixes or for mastering and pressing CDs. While the MiniDisc format is a good, cheap digital medium, do keep in mind that it does perform some very funky data compression and, depending on how you use it, this can occasionally wreck the harmonics and overtones in your material.

Other Hardware

If you're at all serious about production, at some point you're going to need an external mixing desk. A good one to start with is the 16-channel Mackie or perhaps the Spirit 12-channel Folio. There are always a new, improved and cheaper mixers coming onto the market, but as with everything else it's worth shopping around and checking out second-hand sources as well.

If you can afford it, it might also be a good idea to pick up a good-quality microphone pre-amp. This is not to say that the pre-amps in all mixers are particularly bad – the ones in the Mackie, for example, are pretty good – but even many mid- to upper-mid-level mixing desks can have mediocre mic pre-amps.

Monitor speakers will also have a great impact on the finished sound of your mixes, so don't use those three-ways that came with your JVC stereo system. In the affordable range, you could consider models like the JBL and the industry-standard Yamaha NS-10, neither of which sound all that incredible and yet seem to mix very well once you're used to them. The problem with monitoring your material over your home stereo is that consumer speakers have built-in EQ curves and other devices designed to sweeten the sound that they produce. What you want to hear from a mix when you're monitoring, however, is the absolute sonic truth. Pro audio monitors don't lie (well, at least not nearly as much), and it's also worth keeping a pair of really cheap boombox speakers nearby just to reference things once in a while. After you've been mixing for a few hours, your ears tend to go woolly, and you'd be surprised how a mix can sound like the voice of God over good speakers and later like muddy trash over your friend's Audiovox car system. It therefore pays to have at least two sets of monitors: a set of good ones and a set of fairly crap ones.

Session Planning

Without going into a lot of detail about how to plan your recording session, it's worth mentioning a few basic practices that you might already be familiar with. The way in which you actually structure your recording session will, of course, depend on the generic style of the music you want to create and the instrumentation and arrangements involved. However, in most instances, it's best to start by laying down rhythm and bass tracks, either to a click track or a guide vocal, or possibly to a main MIDI track. Once you've got the rhythm, bass and chord parts down, you've effectively established the structure and shape of the song and you can build, layer and arrange from there. The nice thing about Cubase SX is that it makes it easy for you to adjust the mix as you record new parts so that, by the time you've got everything recorded, you've got a mix that will be pretty close to your desired final sound.

Also, while this may be restating the obvious, it's absolutely imperative that you tune all of your instruments with a tuner before you start any recording session. Despite what a lot of musicians may claim, most of us don't have perfect or even relative pitch, and a properly tuned instrument is one of the first key elements you need to get right in order to make a good recording. It also means that you won't run into problems later when you start laying down a track with a new instrument only to discover that somewhere in the previous mix of tracks there's an out-of-tune guitar. (Incidentally, most MIDI instruments are tuneable as well, so make sure that all of your instruments are at least in tune with each other – it will make your life a lot easier.)

The way in which you organise your sessions depends entirely on the line-up of instruments at your disposal, as well as the type of music and the generic sound you're trying to create. Once you get into recording sessions, you'll discover that there are several different ways of doing the same job and that most people will simply choose the one they like best and use it most of the time.

4 STUDIO SESSION 1: LAYING DOWN TRACKS

Logistics

For most serious recording, you'll definitely need an external mixer, and since the mixing desk has always been the centre of a traditional recording studio, you'll want to keep your mixer close to your PC system so that you can operate both without moving from your ideal monitoring position. MIDI keyboards and samplers can be positioned to one side or even underneath your keyboard position, and you can experiment with racking or tiered arrangements. Just remember that nothing should be placed or racked higher than the bottom of your monitor speakers or anywhere between the monitors and your head. Make sure your cables are kept out of harm's way and avoid running mains leads alongside signal cables or you'll pick up ground-loop hum. Don't ever remove any earth leads from any equipment, and if you're using multiplug extension blocks, once you've plugged everything in, make sure you leave it plugged in, as plugging and unplugging your gear will weaken contacts and you could end up with dodgy connections creating annoying pops and crackles.

If you usually work alone, try to get hold of a combined mic, pre-amp and compressor for your audio recording, as these work reasonably well for recording vocals or instruments. Also, make sure you've got a reasonably long mic lead, since you'll want to get your mic as far away from your computer and peripherals as possible in order to avoid picking up hum and fan noise.

While real voices and miked instruments are affected by the acoustic environment in which they're recorded, you can do quite a lot with Cubase SX to enhance, process and fix that sound, so don't panic if you don't have total isolation facilities or you get a bit of bleed-through or background noise. One of the disadvantages of the digital revolution in music has been a sort of compulsive obsession with perfectly pure audio hygiene. Personally, I think that a completely clean sound is over-rated, rather sterile and generally totally inoffensive to the average ear (unless you're an anally retentive audio geek). After all, the natural world is full of interference and unintended reverberation, and rarely – particularly in a live performance – is music heard in the acoustic equivalent of a hermetically sealed environment. Let's face it, some genres of music actually benefit from a lo-fi approach, and despite what you might hear from the cultural prudes, a bit of audio dirt can, in many instances, add an important element of warmth and soul.

TIP

When you record, always record dry (ie with no effects), as effects like reverb and VST plug-ins are extremely heavy on processing power. It's therefore always advisable to add effects after you've laid down your tracks. A general tip for both music production and for Cubase in general is to remember always that less is more and that, just because you have the functionality, you don't need to use it. And when it comes to arrangements and mixes, don't use six violins if you can use two – use only what you need when you need it. Remember, depending on the style of music you play and the way you want your final recording to sound, there may be whole sections of Cubase SX that you'll never bother to use. Don't worry about it. If you can produce a recording that accurately reflects the sound you want to hear, you're probably using everything you need.

Fundamentals Of Recording

In many respects, Cubase SX is as easy to use as a simple analogue tape recorder, with the added bonus that you can record on a single track or on several audio and/or MIDI tracks simultaneously. To begin recording on a track, all you need to do is make one ready for recording by clicking its Record Enable button in the Track list, found in either the Inspector or the Mixer. When activated, the button will turn red, letting you know that you're ready to record. Exactly how many audio tracks (for example) you can record simultaneously will depend on the performance of your CPU and hard disk, although it's always worth remembering that there's no point in recording more audio tracks than you have audio inputs, since this would only result in unnecessary duplicate tracks and audio files.

Record button enabled on Inspector (left), Mixer (centre) and Track list (right)

To begin recording, click the Record button on the Transport panel or toolbar, or use the corresponding key command (default [*]) on the numeric keypad. You can activate recording while you're in Stop mode (from the current cursor position or from the left locator) or during playback. If you activate recording from Stop mode and the option 'Start Record At Left Locator' is selected on the Transport panel, recording will unsurprisingly start from the left locator. If you activate recording from Stop mode and the 'Start Record At Left Locator' is deactivated, recording will start from the cursor's position in the current project. However, if you activate recording during playback, Cubase SX will immediately enter Record mode and start recording at the current project's cursor position. As I mentioned earlier, this procedure is known as a *manual punch-in* and is particularly useful if you need to replace a section of a recording and want to listen to the previously recorded audio up to the recording's start position. All

Punch In and Punch Out buttons activated

you need to do is set the left locator to the position where you want to start recording, activate the Punch In button on the Transport panel and then activate playback from some position before the left locator. When the Project cursor reaches the left locator, recording will start automatically.

You can also stop your recording either automatically or manually. If you click the Stop button on the Transport panel or use the keyboard shortcut (default [o] on the numeric keypad), recording is deactivated and Cubase SX goes back to Stop mode. If you click the Record button or use the key command for recording (default [*]), recording will be deactivated but playback will continue. This is the *manual punch-out* described earlier. If the Punch Out button is activated on the Transport panel, recording will be deactivated when the Project cursor reaches the right locator, executing an automatic punch-out.

As discussed in Chapter 2, with Cubase SX you can also record and play back a loop by using the Cycle function. To create a loop, simply specify the start and end points by setting the left and right locators in the desired positions. When the Cycle button is engaged, by clicking the Cycle button on the Transport panel, the selected section will repeat seamlessly *ad infinitum* until you hit

Stop or deactivate Cycle mode. To record in Cycle mode, you can start recording from the left locator, from before the locators or from within the loop itself, either from Stop mode or during playback. As soon as the Project cursor reaches the right locator, it will jump back to the left locator and continue recording a new lap. When using Cycle mode, however, keep in mind that the overall results of cycle-recording audio and MIDI are always somewhat different. And remember that, if you decide that you don't like what you've just recorded, you can always delete it by selecting Undo from the Edit menu.

The Transport panel showing the Cycle button engaged

OK, that's the fundamentals out of the way. As I mentioned in Chapter 2, all of your recording, editing and arranging for both audio and MIDI will be done within the Project window. Now let's have a look at how to go about laying down some MIDI and audio tracks.

Recording MIDI

As I mentioned earlier, in Cubase SX there's less of a distinction between the way in which MIDI and audio are handled in the recording process than perhaps there was in previous versions. This is generally seen as a good thing, although there have been a few grumbles about the loss of a few working features.

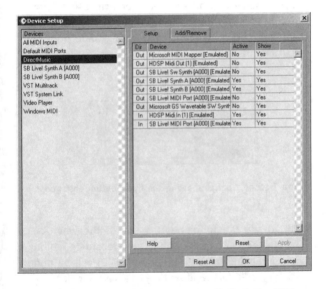

Before recording, make sure you've sorted all of your MIDI settings in the Device Setup menu

Traditionally, many musicians find recording MIDI a bit easier than recording audio, since with a MIDI keyboard, for example, you can essentially record all of the various parts of your musical composition one at a time and then play them back together in perfect synchronisation. As with most things in the digital studio, all of your sounds, tempi, effects and so on can of course still be chopped, changed and altered *ad infinitum*.

Before you begin your MIDI recording session, you'd be wise to double-check the following:

- Is your MIDI interface connected and working properly?

- Have you connected a MIDI keyboard or other controller and a MIDI sound source?

- Is your sound source General MIDI, GS or XG compatible?

Incidentally, if your keyboard or sound source isn't GM compatible, you won't be able to select sounds from the pop-up menus in Cubase SX. To do this, make sure that your MIDI keyboard is connected to the MIDI In of your MIDI interface.

Basic Cubase SX

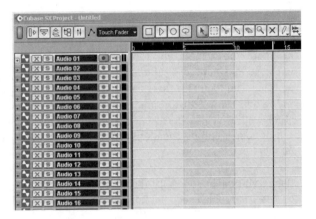

The Cubase SX Project window

If you're engaged in some serious production work, I'll assume that you have at least one or more MIDI instruments at your disposal, each set to one MIDI channel, or that you have one or more multitimbral instruments with each sound set to one MIDI channel. These days, the normal way to work with MIDI is to have MIDI Thru activated in Cubase SX and Local Off selected in your MIDI instruments. By working like this, everything you play during recording will be 'echoed' back out again on the MIDI output and channel selected for the recording track. To achieve this, go to the File menu and open the 'Preferences' dialog box (MIDI page) and make sure that 'MIDI Thru Active' is selected.

Before you start a new recording, and before you start to create a MIDI track, you'll need to open a new Project window. What you'll get is an empty default screen with a number of track options for you to define. Don't worry about the default labels – you can set up your tracks however you want to. To create a MIDI track, select 'Add Track' from the Project menu and then, from the submenu that appears, select 'MIDI' and Bob's your uncle – a MIDI track is added to the Track list.

Adding a track to the Track list

OK, now you'll need to select MIDI inputs for tracks in the Inspector, to the left of the track list in the Project window. To set the MIDI input for a particular track, pull down the 'In' pop-up menu in the Track list and select your desired input. Available MIDI inputs will be listed, and the items shown on the menu will depend wholly on the type of MIDI interface you're using. You can, of course, set each track's MIDI input independently.

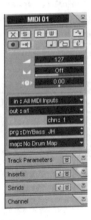

Selecting a MIDI input

Start the MIDI track recording by clicking the corresponding button in the Track list. When the track is record enabled, MIDI Thru is automatically activated, although it can also be set in the Inspector. Once you've done this, try playing a few notes on your MIDI instrument to test the level meter in the Track list and make sure that the MIDI signal is being received loud and clear. If it's not, go back and check that you've set up your MIDI system correctly, as described earlier. If you still have no luck, you'll have to enter the dark and arcane world of MIDI cables.

Once you're satisfied with your sound and signal, set the MIDI output for the track you want to record on by pulling down the 'Out' pop-up menu in the Track list and selecting the output where your chosen MIDI device is connected. Again, available MIDI outputs will be shown, depending on what type of MIDI interface you're using, your system set-up, etc. To actually set the MIDI channel for a track, use the MIDI 'Chn' pop-up menu in the Track list. (Incidentally, if you set the track's MIDI channel to 'Any', it will transmit MIDI on the channels that were used by the MIDI instrument you were playing while recording.)

Everyone will have a different set of MIDI instruments, so I won't go into any great detail concerning wiring and settings. However, to select different sounds, you can send Program Change messages to your MIDI device by clicking the 'Prg' value field in the Track list. You'll find that Program Change messages give access to

Selecting a MIDI channel

128 program locations, and if your MIDI instruments have more than 128 programs, Bank Select messages (set in the 'Bnk' value field) allow you to select different banks, each containing a number of programs. Once you've made your selection, be sure to play a few notes on your MIDI instrument to make sure that your selected sound program is correct, or at least what you had in mind.

Changing a MIDI sound via the 'Prg' drop-down menu

Now you can get down to the recording process, which is fairly straightforward. After you've finished, you'll have a part containing MIDI events in your Project window. Before you start, though, make sure that you set the Metronome for an appropriate pre-count and click track.

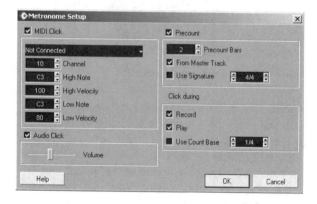

Setting metronome parameters

Set the pre-count for an appropriate number of bars to give you a reasonable lead-in before your song actually starts to be recorded. (You'll also need to set your key signature and tempo to whatever settings you want for your song in the Transport panel.)

Basic Cubase SX

Before you start recording, make sure that the Click button is activated so that the guide click track will play through your speakers or MIDI instrument. You should probably also activate Punch In/Out on the Transport panel.

Selecting tempo and key signature

You'll want your recording to start at the cursor position, so pull down the Transport menu and make sure that 'Start Record At Left Locator' is deselected. Place the Project cursor at the position where you wish to begin recording, then activate Record on the Transport panel and play a few notes on your MIDI instrument. As I mentioned earlier, when you've finished recording, a MIDI part containing all of your MIDI events will be created in the Project window. Once you've finished recording, click the Record Enable button in the area to the left of the track so that it goes dark.

To play back what you've just recorded, move the Project cursor to the beginning of the recorded MIDI part either by clicking on the Ruler or by using the Rewind button on the Transport panel. Then, just like with a normal tape recorder, simply click the Play button on the Transport panel and your recording will be played back. When you've listened to your work of genius for long enough, click the Stop button on the Transport panel. As I said earlier, instead of moving the Project cursor manually each time you want to play back a section, you can use the Cycle button on the Transport panel to get Cubase to play back your recorded parts and events repeatedly, over and over again. All you need to do is click on a MIDI part to make sure it's selected, pull down the Transport menu and select 'Locators To Selection', then click the Cycle button on the Transport panel so that it lights up, move the Project cursor to the beginning of the recorded part and click Play. Once playback starts, when the Project cursor reaches the end of the recording at the right locator, it will immediately jump back to the left locator and continue to play.

TIP

When you record MIDI in Cycle mode, what you actually end up with will depend on which Cycle Record mode is selected on the Transport panel. If you've selected 'Mix' for each completed lap, everything you record is added to what was previously recorded in the same part. You might find this particularly useful for building up rhythm patterns or drum parts. If you've selected 'Overwrite' for each completed lap, everything you record will replace whatever you previously recorded in the same part.

Quantizing

A real plus with programs like Cubase SX is that, once you've record a track, you can quantize it to sort out any timing discrepancies in your playing. Essentially, quantizing pulls together all of those various rogue notes that you might have misplayed while recording and tightens up your timing to match your desired quantize setting.

To set the desired quantize value, go to the MIDI menu and select 'Quantize Setup', as shown at the top of the next page. You will then be presented with a dialog box like that shown at the bottom of the next page in which you can select quantize values for your music. Whatever values you select will remain valid until you change them, and you can continue to record as many more tracks set to this value as you like. Also, if AutoQuantize is activated on the Transport panel (via the AQ button), the notes you record will automatically be quantized according to the currently selected quantize settings.

Studio Session 1: Laying Down Tracks

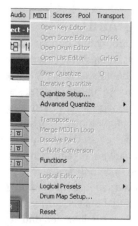

Selecting quantize functions

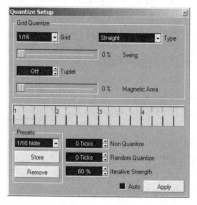

The 'Quantize Setup' dialog box

Recording Audio

Essentially, recording audio in Cubase SX isn't all that dissimilar to recording MIDI, in terms of pure logistics, and since this book is essentially designed as a quick start, I won't go into any great details about the arcane world of Windows audio-hardware set-ups and input/output configurations. Each musician chooses his or her own preferred studio set-up and kit, and to this end I can only advise (again) that you read all of the documentation that comes with your soundcard, mixer, etc, and follow their instructions meticulously. This means that, before I tell you how to record some audio, I'll assume that you've installed and set up your audio hardware, that your audio source (ie mixer, tape recorder, etc) is properly connected to the inputs of the audio hardware and that the outputs of your audio hardware are connected to equipment that will allow you to listen to the recorded audio during playback. I will also assume that you're monitoring your audio source externally so that you can listen to your audio source before it gets recorded into Cubase SX. (Typical set-ups were described earlier, in Chapter 3.)

As with recording MIDI, before you can start recording audio, you'll need to open a new Project window. To do this, pull down the File menu and select 'New Project' and a dialog will appear listing a number of project templates. Ensure that 'Empty' is selected and then click 'OK'. A 'File' dialog box will appear allowing you to specify a location for the Project folder, which will contain all of the files related to your project. This folder will then be created on your hard drive and an empty Project window will appear. At this point, you can set various criteria for your project, such as sample rate and resolution. However, for purposes of simplicity, use the default settings for now.

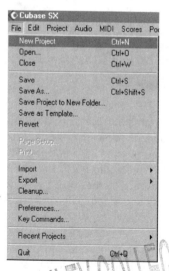

Opening a new project

Basic Cubase SX

To create an audio track to record on, simply pull down
the Project menu and select 'Add Track'. A submenu will
appear listing the various types of tracks available in
Cubase SX, and since here you'll be recording audio,
select 'Audio' to make an empty audio track appear in
your Project window.

Creating an audio track

Before you can start recording, you'll need to decide
whether you want to record in stereo or mono. To make
this selection, click the Stereo/Mono switch in the area
to the left of the audio track. For example, to make
your chosen track stereo, click the button so that it
lights up and shows a double circle, as shown at the
top of the next page.

The next thing you'll need to do is activate and route
all of your various inputs. To do this, simply pull down

Selecting a stereo track

the Devices menu and select 'VST Inputs'. In the window that pops up, you'll see lists of all audio inputs on your audio hardware, enabling you to turn various inputs on or off. From this list, find the input pair to which you've connected your audio source and click on it to make sure that its On button in the Active column is...well, on.

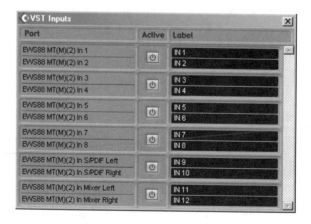

Activating VST inputs

Basic Cubase SX

Now close the VST Inputs window and select 'Mixer' from the Devices menu. This opens Cubase SX's Mixer window, which is used for setting levels, pans and everything you'd set on a hardware mixer. The Mixer contains a channel strip for each audio, MIDI and group track in the Project window, so in theory you should see a single strip of stereo audio channels. Pull down the Input pop-up menu at the top of this strip to determine which audio input should be routed to the audio channel for recording. When you select the input pair to which you've connected your audio source, that audio source will be routed to the audio channel so that it can be recorded on the audio track. For the moment, leave the Mixer window open.

A channel input in the Mixer

OK, the next thing you need to do is to make sure your input level's not too high so that you don't run into clipping. To do this, click the Record Enable button, located next to the fader on the Mixer channel strip. When this button is lit, the level meter will show the input level, as opposed to the level of the playback signal. As you can see here, record enabling the track can be done in the Mixer or in the Track list.

Activating Record Enable status in the Mixer (left) and the Track list (right)

When you activate your audio source, you'll see the level meters reacting. Try to adjust the output level of your audio source so that the meters go as high as possible without going up to 0.0dB, then check the numeric peak-level indicator above the meter in the channel strip.

It's usually good practice to keep the Transport panel positioned at the bottom of your screen, below your

Basic Cubase SX

Project window, as this means that you'll always have access to controls that you'll be using quite often.

Before you begin recording, you'll probably want to click on the Stop button and engage the Cycle function, and you'll also need to click in the Ruler (that black timeline above the track in the Project window) at the position where you want to start recording. When you click here, the Project cursor – a black vertical line – is automatically moved to that position, and recording will start from here.

The Cubase SX Project cursor

You can now start recording. Click on the Record button on the Transport panel and the Project cursor will start moving. Play your instrument and, during the recording process, a rectangle will appear covering the recorded area. This is your *recorded audio event*. When you're done, click the Stop button on the Transport panel and Cubase SX will calculate a waveform image of your recording and display it in the audio event.

Audio events in the Project window

To play back your recorded audio track, move the Project cursor to the beginning of the recorded audio event, either by clicking in the ruler or by using the Rewind button on the Transport panel. Then simply click the Play button on the Transport panel and you can listen to your performance. At the risk of restating the obvious, when you're done, click the Stop button on the Transport panel.

You can, of course, carry on and continue recording audio on the same track or on a new track. Indeed, in Cubase SX, it's possible to record audio events that overlap each other, although only the visible events (ie the events at the top) will be heard when you play back.

You'll probably want to record additional tracks and play your existing track while you do so. To do this, create a new audio track by going to the Add Track submenu in the Project menu and choosing either stereo or mono by using the Stereo/Mono switch in the area to the left of the track. Proceed as before and then, in the Project window, click on the new track's Record

Enable button. (Always make sure that the Record Enable button for the first track is disabled, though, or you'll find you're recording on both tracks at the same time, which could be disastrous.) Now move the Project cursor to the desired start position and click on the Record button on the Transport panel. While you're recording, the first audio track is also played back.

As I mentioned earlier, you don't have to worry if you decide that you don't like what you've just recorded; you can delete it easily by selecting Undo from the Edit menu. When you do this, the event you've just created will be removed from the Project window and the audio clip in the Pool will be moved to the Trash folder, but the recorded audio file won't be removed from the hard disk. However, since their corresponding clips are moved to the Trash folder, you can delete the files by opening the Pool and selecting Empty Trash from the Pool menu.

TIP

Audio files can be huge, so be aware of the sort of real estate you'll be occupying. As an example, for each minute of audio recording at 44.1kHz mono, you'll burn through around 5Mb of hard-disk space for each channel. That means that, if you want to record continuously on a measly four channels for a miserly three minutes, you'll still need a humungous 60Mb of free hard-disk space. Keep this in mind when you start thinking about using a lot of real instruments or live vocals.

Troubleshooting

Although I know I've said it before, when you get into full-blown production, recording digital audio can be a bit like trying to perform an ancient magic spell from a dodgy modern translation of some obscure and dusty grimoire. All the symbols are probably there, the proper ingredients and accoutrements are readily available, but the phrasing and procedural order for completing the great work might have got a bit muddled and obscured along the way. If in the course of your recording session you find yourself confronted by a panoply of unexpected or unwanted demons, just draw a protective circle around your PC and associated kit and ask yourself the following riddles:

- Are your cables and connections faulty, or is it the input signal itself? Is the sound source switched on and active?

- Have you tested your audio card to make sure that it's installed correctly? Could there be some sort of impedance mismatch between your source audio signal and the soundcard?

- Have you inadvertently confused the left and right inputs on your soundcard, and have you chosen the correct input on the selected audio track?

Food for thought or fuel for paranoia? The choice is yours. However, after all that, you should have managed to lay down a few tracks. If, by chance, you've experienced any additional problems, particularly with recording audio, even after trying the various tips mentioned, it's all probably due to the savage and inexplicable intervention of gremlins lurking in the range of parameters related to the audio hardware you happen to be using. But don't despair – the best way to get the sound you want from Cubase SX is to continue to experiment and try out functions as and when you feel you need them. As for all those manuals that came with your soundcard, mixer, MIDI kit, etc, just bung them in the loo and peruse them at your leisure.

5 STUDIO SESSION 2: MIDI AND AUDIO

Once you've got a few basic tracks down, you then need to start thinking about things like the mix – layering instruments, cutting up sections, sorting out timing and adding various effects that will ultimately allow you to create the perfect finished mix. Cubase SX provides an impressive assortment of virtual mixing consoles and effects racks that include sophisticated EQ controls, adjustable reverb, delay, chorus and other fun toys for achieving the exact sound and feel you're looking for.

An important thing to remember with digital recording is that the whole concept of multitrack mixing can't really be separated from the rest of the recording process. In the digital studio, all those neatly packaged tasks common to traditional studios become somewhat blurred so that, in a sense, you're usually building your mix and final sound in a much more fluid and flexible manner. Ideally, this will allow for more artistic control at each step in the process. And best of all, if it's your PC, you're not paying for studio time by the hour.

Basic Cubase SX

Like so many other tools, the mixer windows in Cubase SX have been morphed into a brand new Track Mixer incorporating some of the best features of Nuendo's mixer while pushing the overall functionality that little bit further. The Track Mixer is laid out more like a traditional studio console and looks very little like the mixers in previous versions of Cubase. If you're familiar with earlier versions of Cubase, you'll notice that each channel on the mixer now corresponds to a track on the Project window, with the top-to-bottom ordering of tracks echoed in a militaristic left-to-right formation in the Track Mixer. You no longer have separate mixer windows for MIDI and audio channels, since the Track Mixer now displays the whole lot in one place. You can configure the new mixer's appearance nearly any way you desire, and the new Extended View allows you to set up inserts, sends and built-in EQ from the main Mixer window. In Cubase SX, you actually get five Extended Views, providing either eight inserts, eight sends or four sets of EQ controls, and you can display all of these controls either as knobs or faders, depending on your preference. Even the faders themselves have been narrowed to conserve space.

As you can see from the illustration over the page, the Mixer window is very similar in appearance to a

The Cubase SX Mixer window

conventional hardware console, with a level fader for each audio and MIDI channel strip. The Mixer contains the same number of channels as the number of audio and MIDI tracks present in each current project, and along with each channel's level fader you'll also find a level meter which indicates the signal level of audio events on the corresponding audio track during playback. As a point of reference, keep in mind that with MIDI tracks the meters show velocity levels, not signal levels. Apart from the usual audio, MIDI and group channels, you'll also be able to work with any activated ReWire or VST instrument channels, which are also shown in the Mixer.

Mixing MIDI

To mix MIDI tracks, your MIDI instruments have to respond to volume and pan messages, and if they happen to support Roland's GS extension of General MIDI, or Yamaha's XG, you'll be able to control a whole range of other parameters such as effects, filters and envelopes. While MIDI tracks are also shown in the Mixer and basic mixer operations such as setting level and pan, using muting and soloing and automation are the same for both audio and MIDI channel strips, it's still worth your while to check out the relevant chapter in the operating manual for descriptions of MIDI mixing specifics.

OK, so each audio, MIDI and group channel track in the Project window is also represented by its own channel strip in the Mixer, which you can open simply by selecting it from the Devices menu. It's also possible to specify which types of channel to show and which to hide in the Mixer by accessing additional control bars or menus by clicking the arrow on the top bar of each column.

You can also do this by using the 'Channel Type Show/Hide' indicators at the bottom of the Common panel, which will be lit for visible channel types. Show or hide the desired channel type in the Mixer by clicking on the corresponding channel-type indicator, as shown below.

The leftmost column of buttons on the channel strip – shown over on the next page – is called the Common panel, and this has all your controls for setting things like pan control, mute and solo and channel automation, as well as an edit button, bypass inserts, disable sends and monitor and record enable buttons. Directly above the fader to the right of the pan control is the MIDI input source pop-up and directly to the right of the fader is the level/velocity meter. At the bottom of each fader pod you'll find the MIDI output routing pop-up.

Moving onto the Master section, which usually appears on the left of the mixer, you'll find controls for the master volume, master level meters, and at the bottom the master mono/stereo switch, output routing pop-ups and automation controls. The Master section allows you to control the output level of the main output bus, and with the Mixer in Extended mode, the Master section will also contain the master-effect slots. (This section can be shown or hidden in the Mixer by clicking the Show Master button in the Common panel.) Directly above the Master mixer you'll find the master-effects slots as well.

The Cubase SX channel strip

Steinberg has designed the Mixer panel to look and feel as close to any real-world console as possible within a virtual environment. So, like in the real world, you slide the faders to increase or decrease volume, and each channel has a Mute button to silence the output of selected tracks and a Solo button which silences the outputs of all other tracks shown on the Mixer. As mentioned earlier, all of these controls are now more or less standardised for both MIDI and audio in Cubase SX.

The Master section

TIP

Remember, the level meters for MIDI channels don't show volume levels. Instead, they indicate the velocity values of the notes played back on MIDI tracks, so if you pull down a fader for a MIDI channel that's playing, your meter will still show the same level, although the actual volume will change because the connected MIDI device is set to respond to MIDI volume.

When working with MIDI, use the Track Control effect to adjust parameters on GS- or XG-compatible MIDI devices. As I mentioned in Chapter 4, the Roland GS and Yamaha XG protocols are extensions of the General MIDI standard, providing more sounds and better control of various instrument settings. If your own instrument is compatible with GS or XG, the Track Control box allows you to adjust sounds and effects in your instrument from within Cubase SX. At the top of the Track Control window, you'll find a pop-up menu where you can select any of the available control panels. Users of previous versions of Cubase will notice a slight change in the modes available, which include:

- **XG Effect And Sends** – Effect sends and various sound-control parameters for use with instruments compatible with Yamaha's XG standard

- **XG Global** – Global settings affecting all channels for instruments compatible with Yamaha's XG standard

The Track Control box

- **GS Basic Controls** – Effect sends and various sound-control parameters for use with instruments compatible with Roland's GS standard

- **Off** – No control parameters available

When you're mixing, remember that, if you have several MIDI tracks/Mixer channels set to the same MIDI channel and routed to the same MIDI output, any volume settings you make for one of these tracks or channels will also affect all other Mixer channels set to the same MIDI channel or output combination. This also applies to things like pan settings.

Mixing Audio

Audio-related channels – which include audio, group, VST instrument and ReWire channels – all have essentially the same channel-strip layout on the mixer. However, since audio inputs are never routed to group or VST instrument channels, audio tracks – or *disk channels*, as they're otherwise known – also have an Input Source pop-up menu as well as being equipped with Record Enable and Monitor buttons. You'll also notice that VST instrument channels have an additional Edit (*e*) button for opening the instrument's control panel.

As well as the controls described earlier in this chapter, audio-related channels include three additional Insert, EQ and Send indicators and Bypass buttons, shown at the top of the next page. If, for example, an insert or send effect or EQ module is activated for a channel, the corresponding button here is lit. (Usually, the effect indicators will be blue and the EQ indicator green.) If you click these buttons when they're lit, the corresponding EQ or effects section will be bypassed, indicated by the button turning yellow. Clicking the button again will deactivate the bypass.

In all audio-related channels, the faders control the volume of the channels before they're routed directly or via a group channel to a stereo output bus, with

Channel strip functions

separate faders for the left and right outputs. Use the
Master Gain fader in the Mixer to determine the output
level of the Master bus. Fader settings are displayed
numerically below the faders, in decibels for audio
channels and in MIDI volume (taking the range of values
from 0 to 127) for MIDI channels.

TIP

*If you want to make fine volume adjustments, hold down
[Shift] when you move the faders. If you hold down [Ctrl]
and click on a fader, it will automatically be set to 0.0dB
for audio channels or MIDI volume 100 for MIDI channels.*

In Cubase SX, the Audio Output bus faders usually move
either together or in tandem. However, if you deactivate
the Fader Link switch or hold down [Alt], you can move
each one independently. You can also use the faders
to set up a volume balance between the audio and
MIDI channels, allowing you to mix manually by

adjusting the faders and other controls during playback. A bit later in the book, I'll be showing you how to automate levels and...well, just about everything else in the Mixer.

When you play back your audio in Cubase SX, the level meters in the Mixer register levels for each audio channel. If the peak level of the audio goes above 0dB, the numeric level indicator will then show a positive value above this mark. Cubase SX uses 32-bit floating-point processing internally, which means that your headroom is virtually limitless; even though you're working in a digital environment, your signals can go way beyond 0dB without introducing distortion. So, for the most part, having levels higher than 0dB for individual channels and groups isn't a serious problem in itself, and your audio quality won't be degraded. However, this isn't the case for the buses shown in the VST Outputs window, including the Master bus, which can also be shown in the Mixer.

In comparison, in the output buses, the floating-point audio is converted to the resolution of the audio hardware, and in the audio domain the maximum level is 0dB. Levels higher than this will definitely cause the indicators above the meters for each bus to light up, showing that clipping is taking place and that you're producing real digital distortion, which should be avoided at all costs.

TIP

While overdriving digital audio is generally to be discouraged, in some dance and electronica mixes you'll find that artists have actually done it on purpose to create strangely textured distortion effects. So, as with most things in Cubase SX, just because someone says you shouldn't do it, that doesn't mean you can't give it a try if it seems like a good idea. As they say, serendipity – or even a blatant mistake – can occasionally add an unexpected and positively creative element that makes a recording unique.

Within the Channel Settings window, you can apply Equalisation, Send Effects and Insert Effects to your mix, and you can also copy complete channel settings and apply them to any other channel. As I mentioned earlier, pressing the Edit (*e*) button on an audio channel in the Mixer – as well as in the Inspector for each audio track – will give you access to this window.

When opened, the VST Channel Settings window contains the Common panel, a duplicate of the Mixer channel strip, a section with eight insert-effect slots, four EQ modules and an associated EQ-curve display

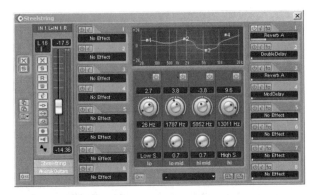

The Cubase SX Channel Settings window

and a section with eight effect sends. Each channel
has its own channel settings, although you can view
them all in the same window if you wish. (Remember,
though, that all channel settings are applied to both
sides of a stereo channel.) Selecting a track in the
Project window automatically selects the
corresponding channel in the Mixer and vice versa,
and if a Channel Settings window is open, this will
immediately switch to show the settings for the
selected channel. This means that you can have a
single Channel Settings window open in a convenient
position on the screen and use it for all of your EQ
and channel effect settings. Alternatively, you can

select a channel manually and change what's shown in the open Channel Settings window.

When mixing, you'll eventually work out a number of cool settings that give you the precise sound or texture you're looking for. When this happens, you'll also find it useful to be able to copy all of those channel settings and paste them onto another channel. In Cubase SX, you can do this with all types of audio channel – for example, you could copy EQ settings from an audio channel and apply these to a group or VST instrument channel to give your mix a consistent sound or feel. To use this feature, simply select the channel you want to copy settings from by clicking its Channel Name field and then clicking the Copy button in the Common panel. Then select the channel to which you want to copy the settings and click the Paste button. And if that isn't clever enough, you can even copy channel settings from stereo channels and paste them into mono channels and vice versa.

OK, let's have a little play with some of the mixing controls. When you record in stereo, you need to determine where in the mix various instruments and vocals will actually appear and how their sound will relate to the rest of the instrumentation. This involves panning a particular channel to a position somewhere between the left and right side of the stereo spectrum. For stereo audio channels, the Pan control governs the overall balance between the left and right channels. As a general rule of thumb, most producers suggest panning bass instruments, bass drums and usually the snare to the centre of the mix. Toms and overhead microphones can be spread from left to right, but don't pan them too hard or it will sound particularly weird. Things like lead vocals tend to work best near the centre of the mix, unless you've got two strong vocals or significant harmonies that you want to spread, while backing vocals can be spread a lot more or dropped further back in the mix. With effects, unless you're trying

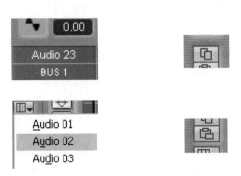

**Controls in the Channel Settings window.
Clockwise from top left: Channel Selection,
Copy button, Paste button, Common panel selection**

Click on the blue line in the Pan control box above the fader and drag to the left or right to change a sound's position in a mix

for something specific, it's probably best to keep outputs from effects such as stereo reverb panned hard left and right to ensure that they have the same level in the mix.

TIP

It's always a good idea to check that your mix is in mono to make sure that the way you've used stereo effects hasn't changed the balance of the overall mix in an adverse manner.

Have a play with the Pan controls and listen to the affect they have on your overall sound. If you want to make particularly fine pan adjustments, hold down [Shift] when you move the pan control, or select the central pan position by holding down [Ctrl] and clicking on the pan control. With audio channels, the output-bus faders determine the levels on each side in the stereo output, and you should also remember that there are no pan controls for VST output buses or the Master bus. With MIDI channels, meanwhile, the Pan control sends out MIDI pan messages, and the results that you achieve will depend entirely on how your MIDI instrument is set to respond to these.

While we're here, why not have a play with the Mute and Solo buttons as well? Have a go at silencing one or several of your audio or MIDI channels. You'll find that clicking the Mute button silences the selected channel while clicking the Solo button mutes all other channels. Solo'd channels are indicated by a lit Solo button and also by the lit Global Solo indicator on the Common panel. (Of course, several channels can be

**Solo (left) and Mute (right) selected on
two different channels**

solo'd at the same time.) If you press [Ctrl] and click the Solo button for a channel, any other solo'd channels will automatically be un-solo'd, while clicking a Solo button while holding down [Alt] will activate 'Solo Group' for that channel. (You can always un-mute or un-solo all channels by clicking the Mute or Solo indicators in the Common panel.)

Mixing Tips

I'll be telling you more about these and other mixing features in a bit more detail in Chapter 8, 'Studio Session 4: Mixing', but while we're on the subject of mixing it's always worth pointing out that a really good mix always starts with a good performance and a well-thought-out arrangement. Despite all the digital magic, if you're not in tune and in time, you'll have one hell of a tedious job building a new and workable performance out of the scrapheap. Yes, you can do a lot to improve small errors, but it's always worth trying to sort out the major problems in the performance at the recording stage rather than trying to fix absolutely everything in the mix. If your mix includes sequenced instruments, it's true that MIDI gives you the opportunity to change sounds right up until the last moment. However, it's still best to have a clear idea of the sound you want before you start since, while modern synths like the Korg Triton sound so extraordinarily rich and impressive on their own, they can give you almost too much choice, and their cool presets can take up all the space in a mix, swamping everything else.

While you're experimenting with the various mixing facilities in Cubase SX, there are a few production guidelines that are worth remembering each time you're working through a recording and mixing session. The simple things are obvious, such as making sure that your microphone placement is optimal and working with your acoustic environment, as well as using the right microphone for the job.

Also, it's important not to over-use EQ. Of course, if your mic placement is right, this won't be much of an issue. Think of EQ as a tool with which to improve creatively already well-recorded sounds and a subtle means of balancing those sounds in your mix.

Be aware that long mixing sessions will make your ears go woolly, so don't abuse them with abnormally high monitor volumes. Take plenty of breaks during mixing sessions and remember that Frank Zappa considered coffee and cigarettes food.

Getting a perfect mix isn't an easy task, and many musicians and producers will maintain that a mix is never perfect. Sometimes the more sophisticated your kit, the more difficult it is to get a mix you're satisfied with, and you should always go with your creative instincts rather than with the potential of your equipment. Just remember that it's fine to experiment with functionality, but it's how your music sounds to you and your audience that really matters, not how you managed to produce it.

6 EDITING AND MANIPULATING TRACKS

One of the best features of Cubase SX is that, in most instances, you can effectively edit your song and its overall sound visually. And once you've recorded your parts you can then begin to use Cubase SX's powerful tools to carry out a wide range of editing functions that will help you manipulate your tracks and arrangement until your song sounds exactly the way you want it to.

As I mentioned in Chapter 4, all of the parts that you create in the Project window can be moved freely between tracks and duplicated as well as split, joined, lengthened, shortened, grouped and much more, even while the music is being played. Cubase also provides a number of specific editors that allow you to look at and work with the contents of each part in detail. When you're using the tools in Cubase SX for editing parts and events, you can in many cases apply additional functions by pressing modifier keys – for example, pressing [Alt] and dragging with the Pencil tool creates a copy of the dragged event or part – so let's have a look at the various default modifier keys available. (Remember, you can customise these if need be by going to the Preferences dialog box in the Editing menu and selecting 'Tool Modifiers'.) For the sake of convenience, while discussing editing in the Project window, unless explicitly stated, all descriptions listed below as 'events' apply to both events and parts.

Selecting Parts And Events

To select an event, choose the Arrow tool and access the Select submenu on the Edit menu. You'll be presented with the following options:

- **All** – Selects all events in the Project window

- **None** – Deselects all events

- **In Loop** – Selects all events that are partly or wholly between the left and right locators

- **From Start To Cursor** – Selects all events that begin to the left of the Project cursor

- **From Cursor To End** – Selects all events that end to the right of the Project cursor

- **All On Selected Tracks** – Selects all events on a track

- **Select Event** – Available in the Sample Editor

- **Left/Right Selection** and **Side To Cursor** – These two functions are used only for range-selection editing

If you want to, say, select all events on a track, simply right-click in its Track list and choose 'Select All Events' from the pop-up menu. You can also use the arrow keys on your keyboard to select the closest event to the left, right, above or below. It's also useful to know that, if you press [Shift] and use the arrow keys, the current selection will be kept, allowing you to select several events. And if the option 'Auto Select Events Under Cursor' is activated in the Preferences dialog box on the Editing page, all events currently touched by the Project cursor will be selected automatically. This can be helpful when you're rearranging your project, as it allows you to select whole sections on all tracks simply by moving the Project cursor. It's also possible to select ranges, regardless of the event and track boundaries, by using the Range Selection tool.

Duplicating Events

To copy an event, hold down [Alt] and drag the selected event to the desired new position. (If Snap is activated, this will determine the exact position at which your copy will be placed.) If you hold down [Ctrl] as well, your direction of movement will be restricted to either horizontal or vertical axes, which means that, if you drag an event vertically, it can't be moved horizontally at the same time. Audio and MIDI parts can also be duplicated by pressing [Alt] + [Shift] and dragging to create a *shared copy* of the part. However, be warned that, if you edit the contents of a shared copy, all other shared copies of the same part will automatically be edited in the same way. I should also point out that, when you duplicate audio *events*, the copies are always shared, which means that shared copies of audio events always refer to the same audio clip. You can always convert a shared copy to a real copy by selecting 'Convert To Real Copy' from the Edit menu, which creates a new version of the clip that can be edited independently and which is then added to the Pool. As you might expect, selecting 'Duplicate' from the Edit menu creates a copy of the selected event and places it directly after the original. If several events are selected, all of these are copied as a single entity while maintaining the relative distance between the events. Selecting 'Fill Loop' from the Edit menu creates a number of copies starting at the left locator and ending at the right locator.

Moving Events

To move an individual event, just click on it in the Project window and drag it to its new position. When you select a number of events, they will all be moved, maintaining their relative positions. Remember, you can drag events only to tracks of the same type, and if Snap is activated, this will determine the positions to which you can move the events.

You'll probably notice that there's a slight delay in Cubase's response when you move an event by dragging. Steinberg maintains that this helps you avoid accidentally moving events when you click on them in the Project window. To prove this, they allow you to adjust the delay via the 'Drag Delay' setting in the Preferences dialog. Functions available include:

• **Move To Cursor** – Moves the selected event to the Project cursor's position. If there are several selected events on the same track, the first event will start at the cursor and the following events will be lined up end-to-start after the first.

• **Move To Origin** – Moves the selected events to their original positions, ie where they were originally recorded.

• **Move To Front/Move To Back** – This function doesn't actually change the position of the individual events, but instead it moves the selected events to the front or back, respectively. It can be a useful function if you happen to have overlapping events and you want to see one that's been partially obscured. This is particularly important for audio events, since only the visible sections of events will be played back. Moving an obscured audio event to the front or moving an obscuring event to back allows you to hear the whole event on playback.

Splitting Events

You can split events in the Project window by selecting the Scissors tool and then clicking on the event you want to split. Again, if Snap is activated, it will determine the exact position of the split. Alternatively, you can split events by selecting 'Split At Cursor' from the Edit menu, which splits the selected events at the position of the Project cursor. If no events are selected, all events on all tracks that are intersected by the Project cursor will be split.

If you split a MIDI part so that the split position intersects one or several MIDI notes, the result will depend on whether or not the option 'Split MIDI Events' (found in the Preferences dialog box in the MIDI Function Parameters) is activated. If it is, the intersected notes will be split, creating new notes at the beginning of the second part. If it's deactivated, the notes will remain in the first part but will appear to stick out at the end of the part.

Joining Events

The action of clicking on an event with the Glue tool joins an event together with the next event on the track. The result is a part containing the two events stuck together. However, if you first split an event and then glue the two sections together again, without moving or editing them first, they'll magically become a single event again. So keep in mind that glueing can create a single event only if the two events are lined up end-to-start and play a continuous section of the same clip.

Resizing Events

Resizing events means moving their start or end positions individually. In Cubase SX, there are three types of resizing modes available to you, and to select one you just need to select the Arrow tool and then click again on the Arrow icon located on the toolbar. This will open a pop-up menu from which you can select one of the resizing mode options. The icon on the toolbar will change shape to indicate the selected resizing mode. Some of the options available from the menu include:

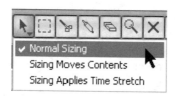

Resizing events

- **Normal Sizing** – The contents of the event stay fixed and the start or end point of the event is moved to reveal more or less of the contents

- **Sizing Moves Contents** – The contents follow the moved start or end of the event

- **Sizing Applies Time Stretch** – The contents are time-stretched to fit the new event length.

Removing Events

Sometimes you just want to get rid of stuff you've recorded and start again. In Cubase SX, to remove an event from the Project window, you can either click on the event with the Eraser tool, you can select the event and press [Backspace] or you can choose 'Delete' from the Edit menu. If you use the Erase tool and press [Alt], all of the following events on the same track will be deleted.

Editors

OK, so the Project Browser provides a list-based representation of the project that allows you to view and edit all events on all tracks. However, there are also a number of more specific editors available for when you want to work on elements of your project in more particular detail. Previous versions of Cubase have all included the now familiar Key, List, Drum and Score Editors, and all of these have survived the transition to Cubase SX with little or no major alterations. If anything, they've all probably benefited from SX's all-pervasive, system-wide multiple undo functionality. The Score Editor now looks like the advanced version that appeared only in Cubase VST/32, and most of the visual aspects of your score can be configured via the Score menu.

You'll find that the score settings in the main Preferences are reserved for general settings in the Score Editor, since any changes you make here will be non-specific. Of the lot, the most significant new feature is the ability to display multiple controller lanes simultaneously in the Key and Drum Editors. You'll find this particularly useful for editing things like pitch-bend information, as it means that you can now keep all of the note velocities visible on screen at the same time. The Mastertrack Editor of previous incarnations is now known as the Tempo Track Editor and provides similar functionality, in most cases, for all things to do with tempo and time-signature changes. Meanwhile, the Master button still appears on the Transport panel and shows you whether or not the Master tempo or the Rehearsal tempo is switched on or off, and a new Project browser – nicked directly from Nuendo – has been added to allow you to categorise every element of an entire project – such as audio and MIDI events and automation data – into a neat, database-style format, replacing previous list-based editors.

Although the Pool has been included in most recent versions of Cubase, in SX it has been given a new and improved organisation and set of features, also stolen straight from Nuendo. Previous users of Cubase will notice that the most significant change to the Pool in SX is that there are now three new Audio, Video and Trash folders. Another nice touch is that you can now organise the Pool more clearly by creating nested subfolders within the Audio and Video folders. While this doesn't affect the way in which files are actually stored on your hard disk, it can make locating clips in the Pool a lot easier.

Here's a brief run-down of how each editor operates.

Pool

This is where all of your files that belong to a particular project are listed. There's a separate pool for each project, so while you're hopefully, metaphorically waving, not drowning, you can organise, convert and audition clips as well as a variety of other things.

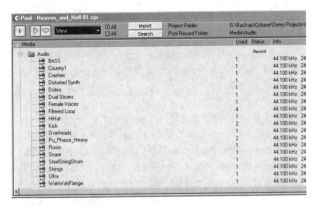

The Pool in Cubase SX

Sample Editor

In the Sample Editor you can view and manipulate audio, by cutting and pasting, removing or drawing audio data. If you use the Offline Process History, you can undo changes or revert to the original versions at any point.

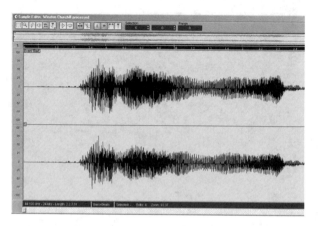

The Sample Editor

MIDI Editors

You can do all your editing of MIDI data with the MIDI editors, which include:

Key Editor

This shows the contents of a single MIDI part, with all MIDI notes represented by boxes whose vertical position corresponds to their MIDI note values, and therefore their pitches. The Controller display shows continuous MIDI events, such as controllers or the velocity values of notes, which can be edited or added to with the Pencil tool.

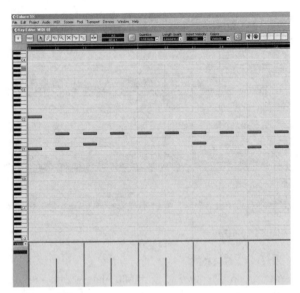

The Key Editor

Score Editor

The Score Editor shows MIDI notes as a musical score and comes with advanced tools and functions to facilitate notation, layout and printing. Unfortunately, for some reason, the Score Editor didn't work properly on the system I was using to test the early-release version – the score would appear, but apparently there was some problem with fonts and I ended up with odd-looking square characters instead of the usual musical notation. I will assume that either there was just some problem with my system or there was a glitch in early releases that Steinberg will get around to sorting out in later versions.

List Editor

The List Editor shows all events in a MIDI part as a list, allowing you to view and edit their properties numerically. The display lists all of the events in the currently selected MIDI part in the order in which they're played back, from top to bottom. You can edit the event properties by using regular value editing.

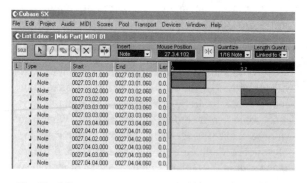

The List Editor

Drum Editor

The Drum Editor is similar to the Key Editor but takes advantage of the fact that, with drum parts, each key corresponds to a separate drum sound. With MIDI, a drum kit is usually a set of different drum sounds, with each sound placed on a separate key – ie different sounds are assigned to different MIDI note numbers so that one key plays a bass-drum sound, another a snare, another a cymbal, etc. Unfortunately, different MIDI instruments often use different key assignments, which can be troublesome if you've programmed a drum pattern using one MIDI device and then want to try it on another; when you switch devices, it's very likely that your snare drum will become a ride cymbal or your hi-hat will turn into a tom, for instance, because the drum sounds are distributed differently in the two instruments and...well, just because MIDI is like that.

To solve this problem and to simplify several aspects of MIDI drum kits, Cubase SX gives you access to drum maps, which basically provide a list of drum sounds with a number of settings for each sound. When you play back a MIDI track with a selected drum map, the MIDI notes are filtered through the drum map before being sent to the MIDI instrument. Among other things, the map determines which MIDI note number is sent

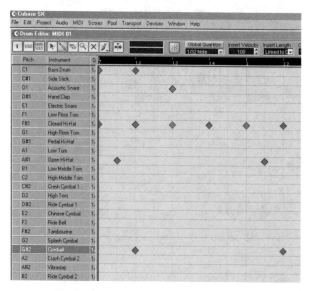

The Drum Editor

out for each drum sound, and therefore which sound is played in the receiving MIDI device.

There's always some variance in the various toolboxes in Cubase SX, and you'll notice in the Drum Editor that there's no Pencil tool. Instead, some imaginative developer decided that we should have a Drumstick tool for inputting and removing notes and a Paint tool

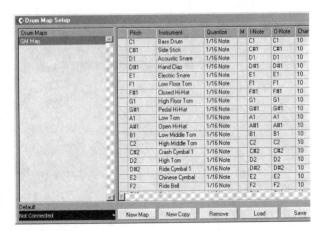

	Pitch	Instrument	Quantize	M	I-Note	O-Note	Chan
	C1	Bass Drum	1/16 Note		C1	C1	10
	C#1	Side Stick	1/16 Note		C#1	C#1	10
	D1	Acoustic Snare	1/16 Note		D1	D1	10
	D#1	Hand Clap	1/16 Note		D#1	D#1	10
	E1	Electric Snare	1/16 Note		E1	E1	10
	F1	Low Floor Tom	1/16 Note		F1	F1	10
	F#1	Closed Hi-Hat	1/16 Note		F#1	F#1	10
	G1	High Floor Tom	1/16 Note		G1	G1	10
	G#1	Pedal Hi-Hat	1/16 Note		G#1	G#1	10
	A1	Low Tom	1/16 Note		A1	A1	10
	A#1	Open Hi-Hat	1/16 Note		A#1	A#1	10
	B1	Low Middle Tom	1/16 Note		B1	B1	10
	C2	High Middle Tom	1/16 Note		C2	C2	10
	C#2	Crash Cymbal 1	1/16 Note		C#2	C#2	10
	D2	High Tom	1/16 Note		D2	D2	10
	D#2	Ride Cymbal 1	1/16 Note		D#2	D#2	10
	E2	Chinese Cymbal	1/16 Note		E2	E2	10
	F2	Ride Bell	1/16 Note		F2	F2	10

Drum Maps: GM Map

Default: Not Connected

New Map   New Copy   Remove   Load   Save

Drum map set-up

with various line and curve modes for painting in several
notes in one go or editing controller events. Not only
that but there are no Scissors and Glue tools available
in the Drum Editor, either.

As in the Key Editor, the mouse-pointer display in the
toolbar shows the pitch and position of the pointer, but
the pitch is shown as a drum-sound name rather than
a note number. The Global Quantize button, meanwhile,
will allow you to select which value should be used
when Snap is on. (Use the Global Quantize value on the

toolbar or the individual quantize values for the drum sounds.) Finally, instead of a Length Quantize setting, you'll find an Insert Length pop-up menu.

Tempo Track Editor

In Cubase SX, you can specify whether each audio and MIDI track should use musical or linear time. Tempo-based tracks follow a tempo, which can either be fixed through the whole project or follow the Tempo track. In the Tempo Track Editor, you can draw curves that determine how the tempo will change over time.

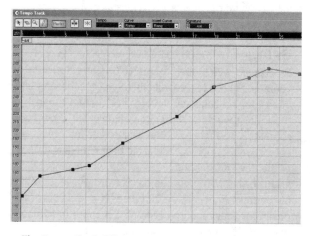

The Tempo Track Editor

For each audio or MIDI track in Cubase SX, you can specify whether it should be time-based or tempo-based. For tempo-based tracks, the tempo can either be fixed through the whole project (referred to as 'Rehearsal Tempo') or vary over time (called 'Master Tempo'). If you want to switch between rehearsal tempo and master tempo, use the Master button on the Transport panel or in the Tempo Track Editor. (Remember that, when the Master button is activated, the tempo follows the Tempo track, and when it's deactivated the Rehearsal Tempo is used.) The Tempo track also contains time-signature events, and these are always active, regardless of whether Rehearsal mode or Master mode is selected.

Using The Editors

Experiment with these various editors and notice the variations in the tools available for each. For example, open the Key Editor by double-clicking a MIDI part in the Project window; the Editor window will show the contents of a single part. (Remember that you can have several editors open at the same time.) The main area of the Key Editor is the Note display, which contains a grid showing MIDI notes as boxes, with the width of a box corresponding to the note length and its vertical position corresponding to the note number (pitch) so that higher notes appear higher up in the grid. The piano keyboard to the left serves as a guide for finding the right note number. At the bottom of the Key Editor window you'll see the Controller display, used for viewing and editing various values and events, such as velocity.

Note that, when you move the pointer in the Note display, its bar position is indicated in the toolbar and its pitch is indicated both in the toolbar and on the piano keyboard to the left, making it easy to find the right note and insert position. To insert new notes in the Key Editor, select the Pencil tool and click at the desired time position and pitch. If you click just once, the created note will be set to the length determined on the Length Quantize pop-up menu on the toolbar. If you wish, you can create a longer note by clicking and dragging the pointer to the right while pressing the mouse button. The length of the created note will be a multiple of the Length Quantize value and the notes will have the Insert Velocity value set on the toolbar.

The transparency of Cubase SX and its ability to let you edit your music at almost any level and to any degree makes it an exceptionally powerful tool. Essentially, anything that you can do in the Project window relating to playback or recording can also be done in the various editors. And as well as being able to go from the Project window to any editor, you can just as easily go from one editor to another or have several editors open at the same time.

Editing happens in real time, so you can edit while music is playing or even while you're recording. If you don't want to record in real time, you can use step recording to input drum tracks or other instruments one note at a time. For example, the List Edit window allows you to view and edit most of the various event types in all of Cubase SX's different track classes. The columns in the list represent different values, depending on each track's class and the type of event, and you can insert any event type, including notes, as well as set the length of each note manually while you're entering it, just as you would in the Key Edit window. Personally, I find the List Edit window rather daunting, and unless you're involved with recording massive arrangements where editing any type of MIDI event requires an extreme level of detail, you may never even need to use it. While the Key Edit window is more accessible, with its graphic approach, List Edit is probably the province of aspiring sound engineers interested in editing non-note events and sysex (system-exclusive) data. However, unlike the Key Edit window, in List Edit you can edit only one track or selected part at a time, although you can edit audio events and MIDI events in fine detail. Whether or not you ever use it is up to you, and if you're using an external sampler you'll already be doing a lot of this there instead of in Cubase.

However, from a musician's point of view, you'll find both the Drum Edit and Drum Map windows particularly interesting and useful here – you might find, for instance, that the more detailed List Edit-type parameters make more sense. In Cubase, a drum map consists of settings for 128 drum sounds which can be named and set to represent particular drum sounds on your synth, sampler or drum machine. You can have up to 64 drum maps in your song at the same time, allowing you to create several different drum tracks, each with its own drum map. Keep in mind the fact that each drum track uses only one drum map at a time and that, when you've defined a sound, all notes already recorded with that sound appear as diamonds on their particular line in the Note display. Initially, the Drum Map window's pop-up menu will contain only one map, the 'GM Map', although you'll also find a number of drum maps included on the Cubase installation CD-ROM.

For each drum sound, you can define what might seem to be a lot of complex parameters, but for most musicians only two are really important for understanding drum maps: the I-note and O-note values. The I-note is a certain key or MIDI note number used for playing the sound, and setting this value determines which key on your MIDI instrument, drum pad or other device plays the sound. (Keep in mind that two sounds cannot share the same I-note.) The O-note value, meanwhile, is the MIDI note number that the sound actually outputs when the instrument is played by you or the sound is played back by Cubase. Let's say that you have a rack synth with some drum sounds in it but they're spread over the range of the keyboard in a way that's inconvenient for your playing style. You can get around this by setting the O-notes in the drum map so that they match the actual notes that play back the sounds on your instrument. If the instrument plays back the bass drum on the C2 key, you could set the O-note value for the bass-drum sound to just that, C2, so that the instrument plays the bass drum. Now you can rearrange the whole 'drum kit' to suit your fingering just by setting the right I-notes.

While each of the 128 sounds of a MIDI device has a note number, this is neither the I-note nor the O-note value but simply a note number used to sort and keep track of the sounds. This might seem like more than you'd wish to know, but only this 'real' note number is recorded by Cubase. As soon as you open a drum part in another editor, the 'real' note numbers will be revealed. If you open a drum track in the List Edit window, or open a folder track containing drum tracks in the Key Edit window, the notes will be shown with their 'real' note numbers, which could make things rather confusing. Therefore, it's always a good idea to edit drum tracks in Drum Edit only. Like Key Edit, Drum Edit also has a Controller display, but this shows only data for the currently selected sound.

While the Drum Edit window makes it relatively easy to create, edit and generally muck about with percussion patterns and even create parts from scratch with the Drumstick or Brush tools, using a keyboard in real time will usually give you a more natural and realistic feel. Try recording whole sections rather than just a few bars that you can loop by copying and pasting. Also, recording a couple of drum tracks at once can give a more natural sound than a number of tracks recorded separately. Of course, this isn't a hard-and-fast rule, and if you're programming some complex breakbeat or other dance stuff then you might decide to program differently. Finally, when you're creating a new drum map, it's often a good idea to start with a map that's similar to the sort you want, if its available, and simply edit it. After all, re-inventing the wheel is never the most productive result of your creative endeavours.

TIP

In Cubase SX, in order to be allowed into the Pool, files must:

- *be AIFF, WAV, SDII or MP3 format*
- *be uncompressed 16-bit or 24-bit files*
- *have sample rates the same as the one used in your song*
- *be mono or stereo.*

AIFF files are most common on the Mac, while WAV files are more common on PCs, and of course you can also import audio files directly into the Project window. If you want to work with MP3 files, keep in mind that these are compressed and can't be played back directly by Cubase. When you import a compressed audio file, Cubase SX creates a copy of the file and converts it to WAV format before importing it. The original compressed file will not be used in the project and the WAV file will be placed in the designated Project Audio folder. Also keep in mind that, while the original MP3 might be quite small, the converted WAV file will definitely be a lot bigger.

Not Fade Away

When you're mixing instruments, vocals, etc, you'll find that it's often useful to be able to fade a piece of music down at the end, or even perhaps fade it up at the beginning. Even within the arrangement you might want to fade a particular part in or out of the mix.

Cubase SX lets you apply fades in a couple of different ways. To begin with, you can use the blue fade handles in the upper left and right corners of selected audio events. These can be dragged to create a fade-in or fade-out respectively. When, for example, you're creating a fade-in, the fade is automatically reflected in the shape of the event's waveform, giving you a visual feedback of the result when you drag the fade handle.

Be aware that fades created with the handles are not applied to the audio clip, as such. Instead, Cubase SX seamlessly switches between the fade sections and the actual clip on playback. This means that several events referring to the same audio clip can have different fade curves. This also means that, if you select multiple events and drag the fade handles on one of them, the same fade will be applied to all selected events. You can also edit a fade in the Fade dialog by double-clicking on the fade or by clicking on the event and selecting 'Open Fade Editors' from the Audio menu. This will open two dialogs if the event has both fade-in and fade-out curves, and if you adjust the shape of the fade curve in the Fade dialog, this shape will be maintained when you later adjust the length of the fade. You can make the fade longer or shorter at any time by dragging the handle, even without selecting the event first (ie without handles being visible). Just move the mouse pointer along the fade curve until the cursor turns into a bi-directional arrow, then click and drag. If the option 'Show Event Volume Curves Always' is activated in the Preferences dialog (in 'Event Display' on the Audio page), the fade curves will be shown in all events, regardless of whether or not they're selected. If the option is deactivated, the fade curves are shown only in selected events only.

Handle-type fades can also be created and adjusted with the Range Selection tool by using it to select a section of the audio event. Depending on your selection, you'll create a fade-in if you select a range from the beginning of the event or a fade-out if you select a range that reaches the end of an event. If you select a range encompassing the middle section of an event but reaching neither the start nor the end, both a fade-in and a fade-out will be created outside the selected range. In other words, the fade-in will cover the area from the beginning of the event to the beginning of the selected range, and the fade-out will cover the area from the end of the selected range to the end of the event. Use the 'Adjust Fades To Range' function in the Audio menu to adjust the fade areas according to the selection range. You can select multiple audio events on separate tracks with the Range Selection tool and apply the fade to all of them simultaneously.

Fade Dialogs

When you edit an existing fade or use the 'Fade In' and 'Fade Out' functions on the Audio menu's Process submenu, the Fade dialog box appears. If you open the Fade dialogs with several events selected, you can adjust the fade curves for all of these events at the same time, which is useful if you want to apply the same type of fade-in to more than one event, for instance. Here's a breakdown of the parameters in the Fade dialog box:

- **Curve Kind** – Determines whether the fade curve should consist of spline curve segments (left button) or linear segments (right button).

- **Fade Display** – Shows the shape of the fade curve. The resulting waveform shape is shown in dark grey, with the current waveform shape in light grey. You can click on the curve to add points and click and drag existing points to change the shape. To remove a point from the curve, drag it outside the display.

- **Restore Button** – Located to the right, above the fade display, this is available only while editing fades

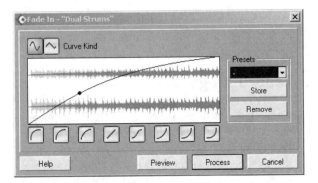

'Fade In' dialog box

by dragging the their handles. Click this to cancel any changes you've made since opening the dialog.

- **Curve Shape Buttons** – Give you quick access to some common curve shapes.

- **Default Button** – Clicking this stores the current settings as the default fade, which will be used whenever you create a new fade.

- **Presets** – If you've set up a fade-in or fade-out curve that you might want to apply to other events or clips, you can store it as a preset by clicking the Store button. To apply a stored preset, select it from the pop-up menu. To rename the selected preset, double-click on the name and type in a new one. To remove a stored preset, select it from the pop-up menu and click 'Remove'. Remember that stored fade-in presets will appear only in the 'Fade In' dialog box and fade-out presets only in 'Fade Out'.

Summary

Of course, as you've noticed by now, some level of technical involvement is inevitable, but believe me, the true secret is to know the essentials of the software and to have a clear idea of the style, feel and sound of the music you want to record. And remember, the great thing about Cubase is that, for the most part, you can choose how deeply into the technical details you wish to go, how much comprehension of various functionality you require for your own individual needs and how much techie-specie you might need to garner from the program's comprehensive manuals. But in the meantime, try your hand at another studio session and see if you can make some further improvements to your recordings.

7 STUDIO SESSION 3: ORGANISING A PROJECT

By now you've probably begun to discover that, when it comes to organising a recording session and laying down tracks in Cubase SX, there's always a number of ways of doing the same job. As you've seen, it's reasonably straightforward to select an audio or MIDI track, press the Record button and end up with a track to work with, but as you come to use Cubase SX more and more, you might find that you want a bit more visual feedback to help you get a fuller picture of what's going on with your song at each stage in the recording and polishing process. For instance, depending on the size of your monitor, you'll probably want to keep the Project window and the Inspector open during recording, and you'll always want access to the Transport panel. You may also want to keep the VST Channel Mixer open to monitor the level of your input signal during recording. (Incidentally, when you start recording seriously, it always pays to save all of the files related to a particular song in the same folder so that, when you need to find them at a later

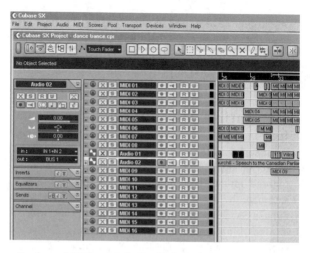

Tracks and MIDI events in the Project window

date, you won't have to go searching all over your hard disk.)

OK, so now you know the basics of audio and MIDI recording and you can record tracks into Cubase. You know what tools to use for basic editing functions and you know how to access VST effects and instruments, and you also know about the internal mixers and how you might begin to mix and process the tracks you've recorded. Now it's time to get back into the virtual studio and have a look at some of these features in more detail. While you're there, you can check out some other techniques and functionality that might improve your creative working practices and help you polish that final mix.

Monitoring The Situation

The term *monitoring* generally refers to listening to the input signal during recording, and this is an important aspect of any session. Essentially, you have a choice of three options: you can monitor via Cubase SX itself, externally by listening to the signal before it reaches Cubase SX or by using ASIO Direct Monitoring, which is a combination of both of these methods. If you choose to monitor via Cubase SX, the input signal is mixed in with the audio playback. The advantage here is that you can adjust the monitoring level and panning in the Mixer and add effects and EQ to the monitor signal, just as you would during playback. The disadvantage of monitoring via Cubase SX is that the monitored signal will be delayed by latency, the value of which will depend on your particular audio hardware and drivers. What this means is that efficient monitoring via Cubase SX requires an audio-hardware configuration with a low latency value. When monitoring via Cubase SX, you can select one of four modes in the Preferences dialog of the VST page. These modes include:

- **Manual** – Allows you to turn input monitoring on or off by clicking the Monitor button in the Track list or in the Mixer

- **While Record Enabled** – Allows you to hear the audio source connected to the channel input whenever the track is record enabled.

- **While Record Running** – Switches to input monitoring only during recording

- **Tape Machine Style** – As the name implies, this emulates standard tape-machine behaviour by input monitoring in Stop mode and during recording, although not during playback.

External monitoring – listening to your input signal before it goes into Cubase SX – requires some sort of external mixer so that the audio playback can be mixed with the input signal. This can be a stand-alone physical mixer or a mixer application for your audio hardware, as long as your virtual mixer has a mode which allows the input audio to be sent back out again (usually called something like 'Thru mode' or 'Direct Thru mode'). The disadvantage of monitoring externally is that you can't control the level of the monitor signal from within Cubase SX or add VST effects or EQ to the monitor signal. However, the advantage is that the latency value of the audio-hardware configuration doesn't affect the monitor signal in this mode. If you do want to use external monitoring, you need to make sure that monitoring via Cubase SX isn't activated as well, so disable this simply by selecting the 'Manual' monitoring mode in the Preferences dialog of the VST page and, well, don't activate the Monitor buttons.

If you're using ASIO 2.0-compatible audio hardware, it will probably support ASIO Direct Monitoring. In this mode, the actual monitoring is done in the audio hardware itself by sending the input signal back out again. However, monitoring is still effectively controlled from Cubase SX, which means that the audio hardware's Direct Monitoring feature can be turned on or off automatically by Cubase SX, just as it is when you're monitoring internally. To activate ASIO Direct Monitoring, open the 'Device Setup' dialog box on the Devices menu and use the 'Direct Monitoring' checkbox on the 'Setup' tab for the VST Multitrack device. If the checkbox is greyed out, forget it – your audio hardware, or perhaps its current driver, obviously doesn't support ASIO Direct Monitoring. If you have any questions about this, contact your audio hardware's manufacturer.

When ASIO Direct Monitoring is activated, you can select a monitoring mode in the Preferences dialog of the VST page, just as you would if monitoring in Cubase SX. Depending on the nature of your audio hardware, it may also be possible to adjust monitoring levels and panning from the Mixer. However, VST effects and EQ cannot be applied to the monitor signal in this mode, since the monitor signal doesn't actually pass through Cubase SX itself. Once again, depending on the audio hardware you're using, there may be special restrictions concerning which audio outputs can be used for direct monitoring. Fortunately, when Direct Monitoring is activated, the latency value of the audio-hardware configuration doesn't affect the monitor signal.

Take Two

Although a single audio track can play back only one audio event at a time, an extremely useful function in Cubase SX allows you to record a number of 'takes' on one track. This means that you can either keep going until you get just the right take of a particular vocal or instrumental track, or you can cut and paste sections from various takes to make a perfect take that you can then use in the rest of your mix. For example, by using Cycle Record mode set to 'Create Events', you'll create one continuous audio file encapsulating the entire recording process. For each recorded lap of the cycle, one audio event will be created and the events will have the name of the audio file followed by the word 'take' and a number indicating the number of the take. Your last take will end up on top and will be the one you hear when you activate playback.

If you want to listen to any of your other takes, just select another take for playback by right-clicking the event and selecting 'To Front' from the pop-up menu that appears. You'll also see another submenu listing all of the other events. When you select the take you want, the corresponding event is brought to the front, and this is a particularly useful feature in that it allows you to combine the best parts of each take quickly by using the Scissors tool to split the events in several sections, one for each part of the take. Since the original take events overlap each other, clicking with the Scissors tool will split all takes at the same position, and you can use the 'To Front' function to bring the best part of each take to the front. This allows you to combine the best sections of each take quickly, using the first line from one take, the second line from another take and so on to compile a perfect – or, at least, the best possible – take in the Audio Part Editor.

A Bit More Audio

As I mentioned in Chapter 4, 'Studio Session 1: Laying Down Tracks', when you record something in Cubase SX, an audio file is created on the hard disk and an audio clip is created in the Project window, with the latter referring to the former. However, an audio event is also created in Cubase SX, and this is what plays back the audio clip. Believe it or not, there are good reasons for this. The audio event is the object that you place on a time position in Cubase SX. If you make copies of an audio event and move them to different positions in the project, they'll still all refer to the same audio clip. Furthermore, each audio event has an Offset value and a Length value. These determine the positions in the clip at which the event will start and end, ie which section of the audio clip will be played back by the audio event. If you resize the audio event, you'll change just its start and/or end position; the clip itself won't be affected.

The audio clip doesn't necessarily refer to just one original recorded file. For example, if you apply some processing to a section of an audio clip, this will actually create a new audio file that contains only the section in question. The processing will then be applied to the new audio file only, leaving the original audio file unchanged. Finally, the audio clip is automatically adjusted so that it refers both to the original file and

to the new, processed file. During playback, the program
will switch between the original file and the processed
file at the correct positions, but you'll hear this as a
single recording with processing applied to just one
section. This makes it possible to undo processing at
a later stage and apply different processing to different
audio clips that refer to the same original file.

As you should also know by now, for an audio event to
be played back in Cubase SX, it has to be placed on an
audio track. This is similar to a track on a multitrack
tape recorder, but in Cubase you can view the event
and move it along the Timeline to another position. You
can place any number of audio events on an audio track,
but only one can be played back at a time. Also, you
can have a virtually unlimited number of audio tracks,
although the number of tracks you can play back at the
same time depends on your computer's performance.

Even though audio events can be placed directly on
audio tracks, sometimes it's convenient to gather several
audio events into an audio part. This is simply a
container allowing you to move and duplicate several
audio events as one. From this point on, each audio
track has a corresponding audio channel in the Mixer –
much like a channel on a hardware mixer – allowing you
to set levels and add things like panning, EQ and effects.

Back To The Fold(er Tracks)

As the name implies, a folder track is a folder that...well, that contains a number of other tracks. Moving tracks into a folder provides a useful way of structuring and organising groups of tracks in the Project window – for example, grouping several tracks in a folder track makes it possible for you to hide tracks and give yourself a lot more working space on the screen, also making it quicker and easier to solo and mute several tracks and edit several tracks as a single entity. They can contain any type of track, including other folder tracks.

Folder tracks can be used in many helpful ways, but a good way of grasping their potential is by considering how your arrangement breaks down, in terms of sections. For example, if you're composing an orchestral piece, you might decide that all of the various string sounds you're using – violins, violas, cellos etc – can be regarded as a section – that is, as a single mixable entity. If you create a folder track called, say, 'Strings' and place all of the associated channels inside it, not only can you temporarily hide them within the Project window but you can also reduce the number of (temporarily) visible channels in the Track Mixer merely by closing the folder. (If you're using a lot of instruments, the Track Mixer can end up being wider than even two 21" monitors can display at once.) It also means that, as long as you've mixed the components of the folder relative to one another, you can then close the folder and use only the fader for the 'Strings' folder track within the Track Mixer to control them all at once.

Folder tracks are created just like any other track. Simply select 'Add Track' from the Project menu and then select 'Folder' from the submenu that appears. Once created, you can move any type of track into a folder by dragging and dropping. For example, in the Track list, click on a track that you want to move into a folder and drag it onto a folder track. When the track is placed in the folder track, all parts and events on the track will be represented by a corresponding folder part that displays a graphic representation of all parts and events in the folder. Since you can move any type of track into a folder track, it's possible to create subfolders by moving one folder track into another. This is called *nesting*, and it allows you to have, say, a folder containing all of the vocals in a project, and each vocal part could have a nested folder containing all of the takes you're using in a subfolder for easier handling. You can hide or show the tracks located in a folder by clicking on the Show/Hide button (the + sign) in the Track list for the folder track. Remember, hidden tracks are still played back as usual, and when a folder is closed the folder parts still give you a graphic representation of the parts and events contained within.

A particular advantage of using folder tracks is that they provide you with a convenient way of muting and soloing several tracks as a single unit. Muting and soloing a folder track affects all tracks in a folder, although you can also solo or mute individual tracks in the folder. Like all other tracks, to mute a folder track (and thereby all tracks within it), simply click the Mute (X) button in the Track list. Folder tracks can be muted in much the same way, but by clicking the Solo button instead. To solo or mute tracks within a folder, show the tracks in the folder and use the Mute and Solo buttons in the Track list as usual for any tracks inside the folder.

As you can partially see in the illustration over the page, the parts contained in a folder track are shown as folder parts, and a graphic representation of the contained events and parts are shown with horizontal/vertical position and length position in the Track list, just like in the Event display. If part colours are used, these are also shown in the folder part.

When several tracks have been put into a folder track, the parts and events on the tracks may end up in several separate folder parts. A new folder part is created automatically if there is a gap between parts and events on the tracks or, in certain circumstances, if there is an overlap between the folder part and an event on a track

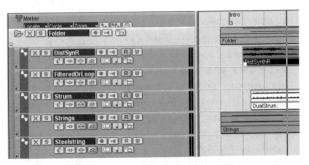

Folder track showing the tracks contained within

within the folder. Within folders, you can perform most standard editing commands like cut, copy, paste and move; the only difference compared to normal part or event editing is that all tracks in the folder are affected.

Multitrack Recording

Among all of the cool features introduced in Cubase VST, there was a function called 'multi-record', which always seemed like a bit of a mystery to dedicated non-manual readers, although it did become a popular subject for Steinberg Technical Support. In a way, Cubase SX has retained this feature and, depending on the sort of music you record, there are occasions when using multi-record, or 'Multiple', will make your life a lot easier.

So what can you do with 'Multitrack' or 'Multiple'

recording? Well, these functions allow you to record a group of performers all at once and still have their music appear on one track each – useful if the audio channels you're about to record aren't related directly but you still want to record them at the same time. If you have a keyboard or some other MIDI controller that can transmit on several MIDI channels, you can record different MIDI channels onto different tracks.

As you should already know by now, to add a track to a Project, simply select 'Add Track' from the Project menu and select a track type from the submenu that appears. A new track will be added below the currently selected track in the Track list, and of course the Add Track menu is also available as a separate item on the Quick menu. For multitrack recording, there is an additional option at the bottom of the Add Track submenu called 'Multiple'. When you select this option, it brings up a dialog box allowing you to add more than one track in one operation. You can decide whether audio, MIDI or group tracks should be created by selecting the relevant number in the 'Count' value field, located in the pop-up menu within the dialog box.

Quantizing

In music perhaps more than anything else, timing is everything. Without it, your whole composition and performance falls apart. That's why one of the most used features in Cubase, no matter what style of music you play, is the Quantize function. Although I looked at this function briefly in earlier sessions, it's definitely worth getting to know more about it on an intimate basis.

Cubase SX offers a number of different types of quantize, but in principle quantizing is simply a function that automatically moves recorded notes to exact note values. If, for example, you record a series of eighth notes, some of them may end up slightly beside the exact eighth-note positions, and quantizing the notes to eighth notes will move the 'misplaced' notes to exact positions. But of course quantising is more than merely a method of correcting errors; it can also be used creatively in a variety of ways and doesn't always have to be used or applied to your entire piece. For example, the 'quantize grid' doesn't have to consist of perfectly straight notes, and if required some notes can automatically be excluded from Cubase's Quantize function. And when you quantize MIDI, only the notes are affected, not any other event types. You can also quantize audio events, and this is a very useful function if you're producing dance music, particularly if you're working with loop splicing.

At its most basic, setting up quantizing involves selecting a note value from the Quantize pop-up menu on the toolbar in the Project window or a MIDI Editor. By default, this allows you to quantize to exact note values only, so if you want more options you'll have to select 'Quantize Setup' from the MIDI menu or 'Setup' from the Quantize pop-up menu, which opens the 'Quantize Setup' dialog box, shown at the top of page 177. Any settings made in the dialog are immediately reflected in the Quantize pop-up menus.

The three quantising types you'll probably use most in Cubase SX are Over Quantize, Iterative Quantize and

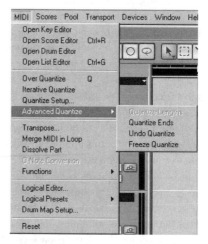

Quantize options in Cubase SX

Groove Quantize. Like I said, with MIDI parts, quantizing affects only the notes and leaves other MIDI messages unchanged. Apart from Iterative, your original notes will always be used for calculating subsequent quantizing, since none of your MIDI data is changed permanently.

Here's a brief look at each type of quantize:

- **Over Quantize** – This is the one you'll probably use the most, since it's the Cubase equivalent of a spellcheck or auto-correct. Over Quantize moves your notes to the closest quantize value without changing the actual lengths of the notes themselves. It also detects if your playing is consistently behind or ahead of the beat and will quantize your chords in a reasonably intelligent manner.

- **Iterative Quantize** – This is a good choice if you want to clean up your timing but don't want a feel that's too rigid or precise. Instead of moving a note to the closest quantize value, this option moves it only part of the way, allowing you to specify how far the notes should be moved towards the selected quantize value. As only notes further away than the specified value get moved, you can allow for a certain amount of loose timing while still being able to tighten up those really dodgy notes. Specify how much the notes

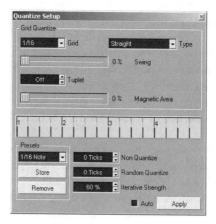

The 'Quantize Setup' dialog box

should be moved towards the grid with the 'Iterative Strength' setting in the 'Quantize Setup' dialog box.

Iterative Quantize is also different from regular quantization in that it's not based on the notes' original positions but on their current, quantized positions. This makes it possible to use Iterative Quantize repeatedly, gradually moving the notes closer to the quantize grid.

- **Groove Quantize** – As the name implies, this option is used to create a rhythmic 'feel' or 'groove' rather than simply to correct errors. With Groove Quantize, Cubase compares your music with a groove pattern and moves notes so that their timings match that particular groove. This feature has improved slightly since Cubase VST, allowing you either to create your own rhythmic templates or groove maps or to use the selection of grooves included in Cubase SX.

Generally, you just need to remember that quantizing affects only MIDI notes, not other event types, and that any quantizing carried out in the Project window applies to all selected parts, affecting all notes within them. In the Key Editor, too, quantizing applies to all selected notes – if no notes are selected, all notes will be affected.

Hitpoints, Audio Slices And Groove Extraction

Hitpoint detection is a special feature of the Cubase SX Sample Editor and is used for tempo-related operations, automatically detecting attack transients in an audio file and then adding a type of marker, or *hitpoint*, at each transient. These hitpoints allow you to create *slices*, where each slice ideally represents each individual sound or beat in a loop. (You'll probably find that drum or other rhythmic loops work best with this feature.) When you've successfully sliced an audio file, you can:

- Change tempo without affecting pitch

- Extract timing or a groove map from a drum loop and use it to quantize other events to the same settings

- Replace individual sounds in a drum loop

- Edit the actual playing in a drum loop without affecting the basic feel

- Extract sounds from loops.

Incidentally, the term 'loop' in this context means an audio file with a musical timebase. For example, the length of the loop represents a certain number of bars and/or beats at a certain tempo. Playing back the loop at the right tempo in a cycle set to the correct length will produce a continuous loop without gaps.

Generating Hitpoints

To generate hitpoints, start by importing your sample into the Pool. You can also use part of an audio track, but if you do, be careful; you're best off doing a bounce on the area you want to work on, as the sliced part will replace the original sample in all instances that use it. If you do a bounce, it's best to use a slightly larger area so that you can snap the loop later on.

Now open this sample/bounce in the Sample Editor and switch to the hitpoint layer. Depending on your material, you might already have good hitpoints, and you can check this easily with the Speaker tool – just click on the area between two hitpoints and the resulting slice will be played. If you're not satisfied with your hitpoints, try the sensitivity slider; most hitpoints sound OK at one level of sensitivity, but there are often some missing at vital points which appear if you increase the sensitivity value – but only after other, useless hitpoints are created. Depending on the ratio of useless to useful hitpoints, either crank up the sensitivity until the missing hitpoints appear and use the Lock tool to fix them in place and reduce sensitivity again or use the Disable tool to click off the useless hitpoints.

Unfortunately, some points never appear, no matter what sensitivity setting you use, but in this case you can manually add the missing hitpoints with the Pencil tool. If you find that the hitpoints are generated slightly too late – a few milliseconds, say – check your source material. This mostly happens with material that was created with samplers where the event starts with noise or just a DC offset. If this is the case, you should use the Move tool to relocate the hitpoints to better positions. If your hitpoints are randomly placed all over the sample, not just at the right places, your sample

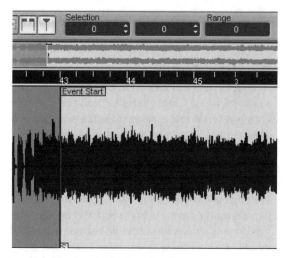

Inserting hitpoints in the Sample Editor

probably contains a lot of different sounds and/or melodies. To fix this, select the right loop and filter the hitpoints via the Use function so that only rhythmically placed ones are used. (You'll probably need to use the Disable tool to disable/enable some hitpoints in order to adjust to swing, for example, or you might even need to draw in or move some additional hitpoints.)

You'll often find that you have to use combinations of the above techniques, so just play around a little until you get the hang of things. Don't worry if you make a mistake – everything you do is in the Undo History.

Adjusting Loops

At this point, you'll probably have to adjust your loop if you don't have a one-bar sample already cut correctly. You'll need to do this now because the selection will automatically snap to hitpoints and, if desired, to zero-crossing points. To go about doing this, hit the Loop button in the toolbar, play the sample and, while it's playing, make and adjust your selection. When you hear the loop you want, hit [P] on your keyboard or select 'Loop Selection' from the Transport submenu in the Context menu. Now you should adjust the number of bars and beats in your selection, as well as its signature, after which the original tempo of your source audio is displayed right next to your selection. Another method is to adjust the loop pointers directly; if your ruler shows bars and beats (ie the default setting), you can compare them to your hitpoints and see if the loop fits.

The basic idea of using hitpoints to slice up a loop is to make a loop fit the tempo of a song, or alternatively to create a situation that allows the song tempo to be changed whilst retaining the timing of a rhythmic audio loop, just like using MIDI. Audio file types that will give the best results when sliced using hitpoints include those where each individual sound in the loop has some kind of noticeable attack; things like slow attacks and legato playing might not produce the desired result. You'll also definitely find that poorly recorded audio might be difficult to slice correctly, and 'normalizing' a file first will improve Cubase's performance in this respect. There may also be problems with sounds that are drowned in a 'smearing' effect, such as short delays.

Using Hitpoints

To make use of hitpoints, start by creating your slices by selecting the Hitpoints submenu from the Context menu and then selecting 'Create Slices'. Now drag your selected sample onto an audio track and it will be adapted to the song tempo. If the sample is already being used in the arrangement, all instances will be replaced and you can open this part and move, copy, mute or delete slices or split the sliced part in the arrangement and work with the slices individually. If you change the tempo, the slices will stay at their rhythmic positions, while if you hear an annoying clicking, enable 'Autofades' to remedy the situation. To do this, open the Inspector for the track in question and click on the Autofades icon or use the Context menu in the Track list to enable all fades. Depending on the change in speed you require, you'll need to select either a fade-in or -out or a crossfade. Select a time between 1ms and 10ms to apply fast fade-ins and slow fade-outs respectively.

When your song tempo is fixed and you've deleted all of the slices you don't want (ie you've muted/unmuted slices until you're sure you don't want them), you can time-stretch the slices by selecting 'Close Gaps' from the Audio submenu in the Context menu. (You can undo this if you change your mind later on.) Afterwards, you can disable Autofades without hearing a resulting click.

Using Groove Templates

To create and use Groove Templates, again go to the Context menu and the Hitpoints submenu, then select 'Create Groove Quantize' to create the groove template. Only one bar can be used; if you have multibar patterns you have to create several grooves, each with one bar selected as the loop. You can choose this groove in the Quantize menu if you want to draw notes by hand. However, with the Curve Draw functions, don't use the Length Quantize function (linked to the Quantize function), as this just presets the curve form.

You can also open the quantize set-up, choose your groove (and save it) and use it to quantize your MIDI or audio events. However, if you just want to quantize a take, you don't need to loop it – just generate and correct the hitpoints, letting your take stay in the arrangement without bouncing it, and in the arrangement select 'Divide Audio Events' from the Hitpoints submenu in the Context menu. Now you can move and quantize directly.

Summary

Hitpoints have been greeted with a mixed response by users of previous versions of Cubase. While it's possible, and indeed easy, to use hitpoints in the Audio Editor for slicing up audio to change the tempo of a loop, it's not possible to use hitpoints in the Tempo Track Editor in Cubase SX as it was with Cubase VST's Mastertrack Editor. Previously, you were able to add metre- and time-based hitpoints and link them together in pairs, while you also had the option of straightening up the linking lines – Cubase would automatically work out the tempo changes required to make certain time-based events fall on a certain beat. This used to be extremely useful for transcribing MIDI recordings if you didn't play them to a metronome, and for many it's frustrating that Cubase SX doesn't work this way. But these complaints come mostly from producers working in video, so it won't be of much concern to most home users. For now, let's carry on with our studio sessions and take a look at some more useful functions for enhancing your musical mix.

8 STUDIO SESSION 4: MIXING

While a lot of people, particularly musicians, focus on the recordings themselves, much of the creativity and personal satisfaction of the entire music-creation process can often come in the mixing session. With Cubase SX you have a lot more flexibility in how you lay down your tracks and how you ultimately mix tracks to create your own personal sound. When you record, basic monitoring facilities can provide you with a reasonable 'ear' for adjusting a range of things such as level, pan and auxiliary sends. And since with Cubase you'll hear exactly what's on your tracks as you progress through the recording, if your monitor mix sounds good, you can be reasonably sure that your final mix will sound great. That's why you should always regard everything you do as being part of the finished product and make it as perfect as possible.

Mixing In Cubase SX

Ideally, as a musician working with Cubase SX, you'll probably want to start the mixing process as soon as your project gets off the ground. While you should have a pretty clear idea of the sound you're aiming for, always allow a certain amount of scope for creativity and synchronicity, depending on the nature and style of your song; if you're working on a dance record, for instance, you need to understand the style well enough to know the elements of the music that your audience demands and should always look for new and different sounds and textures to add to those elements to push your particular style that little bit further.

One of the great advantages of recording with Cubase SX is that you're in control. You're the one that knows how every step of the preparation and recording process is going to contribute to the final mix. This means that, without the interference of an extraneous engineer or producer, the mixing stage should in theory be straightforward and painless. In practice, however, what this really means is that, among other things, you're totally responsible for getting the arrangement right and selecting the right sounds, making sure the musicians are playing in time and in tune and obtaining a good performance from the singer by whatever means necessary. If there's a problem in any of these areas, you can turn a deaf ear to it only for so long – and that's about as long as it takes you to get to the mix. Any problems present in your tracks at the mixing stage will have to be disguised, covered up or fixed, if possible. Remember, this is *your* studio and *you're* the one that has to play producer and engineer as well as, perhaps, writer, performer and arranger.

Setting Up A Mix

A fairly traditional style of album recording involves putting down all of the basic tracks, overdubbing other instruments and vocals and then taking a break for a few days before starting to mix the whole lot. The main disadvantage of working a song at a time, all the way from laying down basic tracks to mixing, is that your ears go woolly after a while and you lose perspective and artistic judgement. Over-familiarity with your song and the recording could mean that you won't be able to judge it in the same way as a punter would. Taking a break between recording and mixing means you can come back to the song with fresh ears and hear clearly which bits need to be brought out and which elements play an important but, perhaps, subservient role.

Mixing is fairly straightforward, but making a good mix is a bit trickier. Since you may not be a sound engineer, using Cubase SX as a musician means that you don't need to know all of the technical details of how to mix. But as a musician, you do need to be able to recognise when something is right and be able to understand what's missing when it isn't.

It's important to keep in mind the purpose of your mix. Is it a dancefloor mix that should sound great on a club PA, or is it intended for CD listening at home? Depending on your style and approach, you might even want to create a radio mix, emphasising some sort of 'buy me' factor – whatever you think that might be – that will attract particular listeners to your release. Just don't think that Cubase SX will guarantee you a place on *Fame Academy* or make you the next Pop Idol. And personally, I'd consider that a big plus.

Formats

Once you've done your mix, you'll probably want to transfer it to DAT or burn it to CD. Some people still whinge that DAT isn't always entirely satisfactory because it reproduces only 16-bit sound, which means that its sound quality isn't any better than the CDs people listen to at home. Personally, I tend not to worry about things that I can't hear. Most of the work that I've done in traditional studios has been dumped to DAT, and the CD masters produced from them haven't been noticeably inferior in any way, shape or form to anything else out there. And despite earlier warnings about using MiniDiscs, in a lot of cases they will also work just fine.

With the range of modern CD burners and various plug-ins and audio software available, it's possible to record, mix and even master a complete album with Cubase SX. I know that for a fact because I've done it myself and have produced a CD which is selling quite well at the moment. Once you've got a CD master, you can either flog it around to commercial record companies or you can send it off to any number of CD producers, who will be able to press and package any number you like at very competitive prices.

But let's not get too far ahead of ourselves. Cubase SX still has a lot of functionality you might find useful during both recording and mixing, so first have a crack at this final studio session and see what else you can do.

Channel Settings

The Channel Settings window in the Mixer is used for adding effects and EQ to individual audio channels. Each audio channel has its own Channel Settings window, and when using the 'Extended Channel Strip' viewing option the upper panel can be set to show different views for each audio-channel strip. Select what to display for each channel by using the View Options pop-up menu at the top of each channel strip.

Channel settings are used to apply EQ, send effects and insert effects and to copy complete channel settings and apply them to other channels. In each case, all channel settings are applied to both sides of a stereo channel. Use the Initialise Channel button at the bottom of the Channel Settings Common panel to reset a channel to the default setting. Default settings in Cubase SX are as follows:

- All EQ, insert and send effect settings are deactivated and reset

- Solo/mute is deactivated

- The fader is set to 0dB

- Pan is set to the centre position.

Each EQ module contains a fully parametric one-band equaliser with the following parameters:

- Gain – Governs the amount of boost or attenuation around the set frequency. The range is +/–24dB.

- Frequency – The centre frequency for the equalisation. Around this frequency, the sound will be boosted or attenuated according to the Gain setting. The range is 20Hz–20kHz.

- Q – Determines the width of the frequency band

EQ section of the Channel Settings window with four modules activated

to be affected around the centre frequency. The narrower the frequency band, the more drastic the effect of boost or attenuation. For the leftmost and rightmost EQ modules, the following special modes are available:

1 If the Q value for the leftmost EQ module is set to minimum, it will act as a low shelving filter

2 If the Q value for the leftmost EQ module is set to maximum, it will act as a high-pass filter

3   If the Q value for the rightmost EQ module is set to minimum, it will act as a high shelving filter

4   If the Q value for the rightmost EQ module is set to maximum, it will act as a low-pass filter.

More On EQ

As any producer will tell you, EQ can make or break a mix. Just as a painter will mix primary colours to accentuate certain areas of a painting and draw the eye across the canvas, so too the producer will mix high, low and mid-range frequencies to achieve subtle colourings of tone that any good mix demands. When you listen back to one of your mixes, two or more sounds operating in the same frequency can often combine in synergy to create a new sound that is greater than the sum of its parts. This blending of sound creates new timbres as well as forcing sounds apart, and the separation of sounds is particularly important in most dance music as a lot of low frequencies infringe on each other's wavelength – for example, bass lines and kick drums. Similarly, a lot of jungle producers will pitch up their drum loops to allow low basses to sit comfortably in the mix. The same applies to mid-range sounds – snares, hi-hats and bongos all tend to occupy a similar wavelength and will need to stand out from each other.

EQ can vastly affect the character of a sound, but if it's used subtly the presence of a sound can be changed without its tonal quality being affected, and this is the key to creating the spacious mixes we're all familiar with. And just as it is with effects, with EQ less is more, so always try to cut frequencies before you have a go at boosting them.

Although some people insist on adding EQ while recording, as a general rule it's best not to. One good reason for this is that, when you create a mix and find out that it's not what you were hoping for, you can go back to a blank sound canvas by resetting your EQ levels and starting again. Another reason is that there's no way you can really know what EQ a sound finally needs until you hear it in context with the rest of a mix, and trying to EQ an already EQ'd sound can create some ugly noises. Remember, some sounds in your mix will have to take a back seat and won't be heard on their own, so why record them with heavy EQ as if they were up-front solos?

Frequencies

As a musician, you may or may not be interested in delving into a lot of techie detail, but when it comes to EQ it's definitely worth knowing a little about frequency settings for particular instruments. This will at least give you an idea of where to start with your EQ settings in Cubase, although you don't have to worry too much about whether or not you actually understand the science. To begin with, an instrument's sound is made up of a fundamental frequency, the musical note itself and harmonics, even when only a single note is played, and it's these harmonics that give the note its unique character. If you use EQ to boost the fundamental frequency, you simply make the instrument louder and don't bring it out in the mix. You should also note that a particular frequency – 440Hz, say – corresponds directly to a musical note on the scale (which, in the case of 440Hz, is the A above middle C, hence the tuning reference 'A-440'). Boosting the harmonic frequencies, on the other hand, boosts the instrument's tonal qualities and can therefore provide it with its own space in the mix. Below are some useful frequencies for various instruments:

- **Voice** – Presence, 5kHz; sibilance, 7.5-10kHz; boominess, 200-240kHz; fullness, 120Hz

- **Electric Guitar** – Fullness, 240Hz; bite, 2.5kHz; air/sizzle, 8kHz

- **Bass Guitar** – Bottom, 60–80Hz; attack, 700Hz–1kHz; string noise, 2.5kHz

Basic Cubase SX

- **Snare Drum** – Fatness, 240Hz; crispness, 5kHz

- **Kick Drum** – Bottom, 60–80Hz; slap, 4kHz

- **Hi-Hat And Cymbals** – Sizzle, 7.5–10kHz; clank, 200Hz

- **Toms** – Attack, 5kHz; fullness, 120–240Hz

- **Acoustic Guitar** – Harshness/bite, 2kHz; boominess, 120–200Hz; cut, 7–10kHz

TIPS

Here are some general tips for getting a better overall sound:

- *Always listen to the whole track dry, with no effects, no EQ, nothing. This will help you determine were things want to sit. Of course, if the song you're mixing utilises processed samples, you won't be able to do this, although a relatively effective way of reducing effects on pre-processed samples is to use a limiter or some form of compression. You can also target the frequency band in which the sample is most effected and reduce the gain, although this can lead to unwanted tonal change.*

- *Thin out pads, backing vocals and acoustic-guitar*

parts with EQ. Perversely, this dramatises the dynamics rather than diminishing them.

- *Smoothe the curve. Although not to everyone's taste, this is definitely familiar as the radio-friendly 'pro sound' of most modern records. The polished feel seems to rest in the mid band, with producers tending to cut frequencies between 200Hz and 4kHz, chopping the most in the 600Hz–1kHz region.*

OK, forget the techie crap. On a graphic equaliser like the one you have in Cubase SX, EQ carried out like this forms a smooth upside-down curve which you can draw in graphically. Professional producers take down the mid range, as middle frequencies have a habit of tiring the ear and blocking the finer frequencies. (This holds especially true on tracks with a profusion of guitar.) The 'edge' that's apparently so desirable is not achieved by boosting the mid range – which seems natural – but by tweaking the top and bottom frequencies so that they interact with contrast.

TrueTape

While digital audio recording has many benefits, some musicians have expressed the opinion that digital sound always tends to be somewhat sterile and cold when compared to high-quality analogue recordings, and indeed, a few years ago, Neil Young was particularly outspoken about the evils of digital sound. However, TrueTape claims to remedy this problem by recreating that good old 'open-fire' sound of analogue tape saturation at the recording stage. TrueTape was first introduced in Cubase VST version 5, offering a unique Steinberg technology that emulates the behaviour of a professional analogue tape recorder. If you're particularly into acoustic music, you might want to play around with this – as long as your system can handle it.

TrueTape produces *32-bit float files*, and all of the hard-disk and processor-speed considerations of the regular 32-bit format apply here. Unlike the regular 32-bit mode, however, you can make use of the TrueTape

TrueTape analogue-tape emulator

mode even if your audio hardware only supports 16-bit resolution, because the TrueTape feature converts the signal to 32-bit float format and adds audio information in the floating-point domain.

To begin, simply pull down the Devices menu and select 'TrueTape', using the Drive control to adjust the amount of tape saturation effect to your liking. If you're monitoring through Cubase SX, you'll hear how the changes colour the sound of the monitored signal, allowing you to try out the settings before actually recording. There's a pop-up menu above the TrueTape panel that allows you to select one of four Drive presets if you want to effect quick changes. These contain no hidden parameters, so selecting the '24dB Super Saturation' preset is the same as moving the Drive control all the way to the right. (Note that any adjustments you make to the Drive control are automatically applied to the selected preset.) You can also rename a preset by double-clicking and typing in a new name. Raising the Drive level will also raise the level in the audio file and will allow you to reach 0.0dB clipping on the input-level meters easily. However, unlike when recording in 16-bit format, this is nothing to worry about; Steinberg say that it's virtually impossible to get digital distortion in a 32-bit float file.

Pods And Pans

As I mentioned briefly earlier on, when you're mixing, you've got to decide where in the mix you want each of your instruments, vocals or other sounds to be positioned. This involves panning sounds and instruments to appropriate positions in the stereo mix in order to achieve the desired level of depth and texture. Although panning can be used quite creatively, as a general rule vocals, bass drum, bass instruments and often snare drum are usually panned to the centre. (In some types of music, though, you might want to pan the snare slightly off-centre.) Vocals can also be panned a little to the left or right, but they tend to sound better if there's a balancing vocal or similar instrument panned to the opposite side. Other instruments, like guitars, brass, keyboards and backing vocals, can be panned to either side. And remember to pan stereo effects like reverb fully left and right if your want to create width in your mix. Of course, you can pan any instrument, vocal or pad sound back and forth in your mix, depending on the effect and degree of movement you're trying to achieve.

You should be aware that, in the Project Setup dialog box, there's a pop-up menu named 'Stereo Pan Law', and from this you can select one of three pan modes. This is all related to the arcane fact that, without power compensation, the power of the sum of the left and right sides will be higher (ie louder) if a channel is panned to the centre than if it's panned to the left or right. To remedy this, the Stereo Pan Law setting allows you to attenuate signals panned to the centre by –6dB or –3dB (the default setting). Selecting the odB option effectively turns off 'Constant-Power Panning'. Experiment with the modes to see which fits best in a given situation.

TIPS

- Don't rely on the pan controls to keep your sounds separate; try to get your mix working in mono first and then start panning the various elements. After you get a rough balance in mono using no EQ, you can then start to play around with the fine tuning.

- When you're actually recording, try to make your up-front sounds slightly brighter while keeping background and supporting sounds less bright. Since it's always easier to cut frequencies using EQ than to add them later, just make sure you've got enough top end in your various recordings.

- To keep that contrast in your mix, don't process everything. If you do, you'll just end up with a muddy cacophony of competing sounds, or something that sounds vaguely like hip-hop.

Pods

As studios become more compact, solutions for instrument recording follow suit. At present, manufacturers offer a competitive range of amp-modelling hardware and software that simulates the 'genuine' sounds of an amp, including effects. This means that you don't have to mic up any hardware and also means huge savings in terms of space and money.

The current favourite models are those in the Pod series created by Line6. A guitar and a bass Pod can be had for around £200 ($315) each, and each unit offers pre- and post-EQ effects, serious EQ and a preset range of classic amp models. It's also possible for you to create your own patterns and models, which means that the classic Marshall valve you've always wanted can be created with a few tweaks.

An alternative to the Pod system can be found in the J-Station, manufactured by Johnson Amplification. This gives guitar and bass modelling along with acoustic-guitar simulation. Both systems are fully programmable.

Automation

For all the idlers out there, it's probably comforting to know that virtually every mixer and effect parameter in Cubase SX can be automated. You can do this either by manually drawing curves on automation subtracks in the Project window or by using the Write/Read functions and adjusting parameters in the Mixer itself. There's no real difference between the two techniques in terms of how the automation data is applied; the methods differ only in the way in which the automation events are created, either by being manually drawn in or recorded. Any applied automation data will be reflected in the Mixer, by a moving fader and a corresponding automation track curve. In Cubase SX, you can completely automate your mix, and the following parameter settings can be recorded automatically or drawn in on automation subtracks.

Essentially, in Cubase SX, there are three types of automation tracks available: channel-automation tracks, plug-in automation tracks and a master automation track. There's one automation track for every audio, group and MIDI track, and also one for each activated ReWire and VST instrument channel. This automation track has a number of automation subtracks, one for each channel setting available, and each channel's insert-effect program selection and effect-parameter setting is handled by the channel automation track. For MIDI tracks, all track, MIDI send and insert-effect parameter settings are also handled by the channel-automation track.

There's one plug-in automation track for each automated

send and master effect and one for each automated VST instrument. These tracks have a number of automation subtracks, one for each parameter of each automated effect and VST instrument.

For each project, there's only one master automation track, and this track can have any number of automation subtracks, just like a single audio track. The Master Gain parameter controls all of the bus-output levels and the send effects' 'master' input levels. In Cubase SX, automation subtracks are not separate tracks but rather separate 'views' of the same automation track, showing one automation parameter at a time.

For each audio and group track, you can automate:

- Volume

- Pan left to right

- Pan front to rear

- Mute

- EQ Master Bypass

- FX Send Bypass

- Settings for four EQ modules (Enable, Freq, Quality and Gain)

- Eight effect-send On/Off switches

- Eight effect-send levels

- Eight effect-send Pre/Post switches

- Surround-pan parameters (if used)

- Eight insert-effect program selection and effect parameters (if insert effects are used)

Meanwhile, from the master automation track, you can automate the following:

- Master gain

- Left and right levels for all output buses

- Send effects 'master' input levels

If audio effects are used, for each plug-in automation track you can automate the following:

- Send-effect program selection and effect parameters

Basic Cubase SX

- Master-effect program selection and effect parameters

- VST instrument program selection and parameters

(Keep in mind that there's one plug-in automation track for each automated send effect, master effect and VST instrument.)

For each MIDI track you can also automate:

- Volume

- Pan

- Mute

- Track parameters On/Off switch

- Transpose

- Velocity shift

- Random 1-2 Min/Max/Target

- Range 1-2 Min/Max/Target

- Four insert-effect On/Off switches

- Four send-effect On/Off switches

- Four MIDI insert-effect parameters (if used)

- Four MIDI send-effect parameters (if used)

TIP

When you're editing automation data in the Controller Editor, it's possible to display two or more channels simply by shift-clicking on them in the panel on the left-hand side. If you're working with stereo or group channels, for instance, you'll need to shift-click in order to display both the left and right channels. Using the Crosshairs and Pencil tools, you can draw automation data in all displayed channels simultaneously by holding down [Ctrl] + [Alt].

VST System Link

VST System Link is a new feature in Cubase SX that provides a network system for digital audio that allows you to have several computers working together in one large system. Unlike conventional networks, it doesn't require a boring plethora of Ethernet cards, hubs or CAT-5 cables; instead, it uses the kind of digital-audio hardware and cables you probably already have kicking around your studio. VST System Link has been designed to be simple to set up and operate while still providing enormous flexibility and performance gains in use. It's capable of linking computers in a ring network, where the System Link signal is passed from one machine to the next, eventually returning to the first machine, and the networking signal can be sent over any type of digital-audio cable, including S/PDIF, ADAT, TDIF and AES, as long as each computer in the system is equipped with a suitable ASIO-compatible audio interface.

So why, you may ask, would you want to link up two or more computers? Well, the added computer power this would give you could open vast vistas of possibilities. For example, you could dedicate one computer to running VST instruments while recording audio tracks on another. If you happened to need lots of audio tracks, you might simply add tracks on another computer. Or you could have one computer serving as a virtual effects rack, running nothing but processor-intensive send-effect plug-ins. And since you can use VST System Link to connect different VST System Link applications on different platforms, you can take advantage of effect plug-ins and VST instruments that are specific to certain programs or platforms.

To use VST System Link, you'll need at least two or more computers. Because Cubase SX is clever, these can be of the same type or use different operating systems. This means you can link an Intel-based PC to an Apple

Mac without problems, as long as each has audio hardware with specific ASIO drivers installed. The audio hardware must also have digital inputs and outputs and, of course, in order to be able to connect up the computers, their digital connections must be compatible. You'll need at least one digital-audio cable for each computer in the network and the VST System Link host application installed on each computer.

At the time of writing, VST System Link is implemented for Cubase SX, Nuendo 1.6 and Cubase 5.1 (System Link version), and any VST System Link applications can connect to each other. On top of that, Steinberg recommend that you use a KVM (Keyboard, Video, Mouse) switchbox.

OK, so what's a KVM switchbox? Well, if you want to set up a multi-computer network, or even a small network in a limited space, it's a good idea to invest in one of these switchers, which allow you to use the same keyboard, monitor and mouse to control each computer in the system and switch between computers very rapidly. KVM switchers aren't too expensive and are very easy to set up and operate. It you decide not to go this route, the network will function just the same, but you might end up doing a lot of jumping from one machine to the other while setting up.

And Then…

There are a few more things to keep in mind during the mixing phase of your project, and if I'm repeating myself here then it's probably because it's important (although a touch of early senility shouldn't be ruled out…).

To begin with, don't mix at a constantly high volume. For that matter, don't constantly mix at the same volume. Check your mix frequently using a very low volume and at various mid-level volumes, and every now and then crank it up to hear how things hit hard. Look at your speakers to make sure you're not overdriving them.

When the mix is finished, you should listen to it from start to finish at a high level, turning the volume down again if you need to make further alterations. Your ears can get tired, woolly and even damaged if you listen to loud music for long periods, causing you to hear a muffled version of the sound that you're listening to. OK, maybe that sounds like your parents blathering on about the evils of rock music, but believe me, you don't want to mess with your ears. If you're a musician, you need to keep them in the best possible condition.

Finally, a well-arranged and well-tracked song shouldn't require a great deal of fader-riding. You might have to bring up a lead instrument here and there, but that's all.

9 PLUG-INS AND VST INSTRUMENTS

VST is now the most common native audio plug-in and was actually pioneered by Steinberg, the manufacturer of Cubase SX. With a format that avoids platform incompatibility, VST plug-ins are available in both PC and Mac versions and provide help in handling all of the usual studio effects such as compression, limiting, gating, reverb, echo, chorus and flanging, and there's also an increasing range of plug-ins coming onstream for things like pitch correction, applying creative or gratuitous distortion, vocoding, denoising, click suppression, spectral enhancement and other such esoteric functions. As is common with conventional mixers, effects such as reverb and echo can be used in an effects-send-and-return loop on the virtual mixer so that a single plug-in can be applied to as many channels as needed without soaking up exceptional amounts of processing power. However, other plug-ins, such as compressors or equalisers, still have to be used on a per-channel basis and must be patched in via controls in much the same way as you would patch them in on a traditional console.

Cubase SX continues to build on the collection of plug-ins that Steinberg licensed to third-party developers in VST version 5.1, with a little help from a new blue interface and a few notable additions. Newly bundled plug-ins that were previously sold separately include the useful DeEsser from SPL and Craig Anderton's funky QuadraFuzz. In the VST instrument cupboard, SX has kept most of the plug-ins from 5.1 but has wisely chosen to ditch the dodgy-sounding Universal Sound Module for General MIDI. For versatility at producing bass, pad, poly lead and effects patches, Steinberg has added a new virtual analogue synth called A1, developed by Waldorf. Since SX seems to have finally overcome the latency problems that dogged earlier versions of Cubase, all of these VST instruments now seem to perform faultlessly. Well, nearly faultlessly.

VST Instruments

VST instruments are software synthesisers or other sound sources that can be contained within Cubase SX. They're played internally via MIDI and their audio outputs appear on separate channels in the Mixer, allowing you to add effects or EQ just as you can with other audio tracks. While a reasonable assortment of VST instruments are included with Cubase SX, a growing number of others can be purchased separately from Steinberg and other manufacturers.

While the limitation of eight send effects and eight master effects found in earlier versions of Cubase is still in place, SX now allows you to run a maximum of 32 VST instruments simultaneously, depending on the capacity of your processor. Since most VST instruments are multitimbral and have multiple outlets, using all of the possible virtual instrument channels available to you would be downright silly, even if you could find a PC powerful enough to run them all. Some VST MIDI windows such as the Arpeggiator and IPS have been left out of SX as well, but in exchange you've now got an open-ended MIDI plug-in architecture at your disposal with which you can format other plug-ins.

VST instruments can be accessed from the Devices menu, and the default 'rack' that appears can contain up to 32 VST instruments. However, the maximum number of instruments depends on your computer's performance and the complexity of the instruments selected. VST instruments that are now bundled with Cubase SX include:

- CS40

- JX 16

- LM-9

Basic Cubase SX

- Neon

- LM-7, a reasonable 24-bit drum machine that has up to 12 voices, compared with LM-9's nine voices, and receives MIDI in Omni mode (ie on all MIDI channels). When you're using it, you don't need to select a MIDI channel to direct MIDI to LM-7, and the unit responds to MIDI Note On and Note Off

LM7 VST synth plug-in

messages. The plug-in comes with six sets of drum sounds, with 'Compressor', '909' and 'Percussion' loaded as the default sounds, while 'Modulation', 'Fusion' and 'DrumNbass' can be loaded by selecting Load Bank from the File menu and opening the file named 'lm7_second_set.fxb', which you'll find located in the 'Drums' subfolder of the folder named 'VSTplugins'. Compressor features samples of an acoustic drum kit, 909 features classic analogue drum-machine sounds and Percussion, as it says on the tin, features various percussion sounds.

- A1, a particularly good dual-oscillator software synthesiser originally developed by and licensed from Waldorf. The A1 is essentially a polyphonic synth unit with up to 16 voices, multimode filters including low-pass, bandpass, high-pass and notch filters and PWM (Pulse Width Modulation). The unit also includes FM (Frequency Modulation), a ring modulator and a built-in stereo chorus/flanger effect. A1 receives MIDI in Omni mode, on all MIDI channels, so you won't need to select a MIDI channel to direct MIDI to the unit. And, of course, the unit responds to MIDI controller messages.

The keyboard shows incoming MIDI note data as if played by invisible hands and can be 'played' by

A1 VST synth plug-in

clicking on it with the mouse. However, if you're playing it in this way, the velocity that's produced will be fixed and you won't actually be able to record anything.

- VB1, a reasonably mediocre virtual bass instrument built on somebody's idea of real-time physical-modelling principles.

  OK, it's not got the class of a 1962 pre-CBS Fender Jazz bass, but VB1, which has had a slightly different-coloured face-lift since appearing in Cubase version 5, still sort of looks like a fairly funky virtual bass.

VB1 is polyphonic, able to play up to four voices and receives MIDI in Omni mode (ie on all MIDI channels). As on a 'proper' electric bass, the Volume control regulates the volume and the Damper switch controls the length of time that the string vibrates after being plucked. You can adjust the position of the pick-up and by dragging the 'mic' left or right, thus changing the tone; positioning it towards the bridge position produces a hollow sound that

VB1 virtual bass VST plug-in

emphasises the upper harmonics of the plucked string while moving it towards the neck position makes the tone fuller and warmer.

Meanwhile, the 'pick' position determines the point along the length of the string where the initial pluck is made and controls the roundness of the tone, just as the pick does when playing a real guitar. The Wave Morph function selects the basic waveform used to drive the plucked string model, and be aware that this parameter can drastically change the character of the sound produced; the control smoothly morphs through the waves, so if you're not careful you might end up creating sounds that have no relation to a bass guitar. Then again, there might be times when you'd want to do that.

All things considered, the bass sounds from the VB1 aren't all that wonderful, and with this plug-in it's probably a case of 'nice interface, pity about the sound'. You'll probably get a better bass sound out of Neon (although this might just be my own personal taste).

To access a VST instrument, open the Devices menu and select an unused MIDI track in the Project window. Pull down the Output pop-up menu for the MIDI track

Selecting VST instruments from the Devices menu

in the Track list or in the Inspector. The pop-up menu will now contain an additional item with the name of the activated VST instrument. Once you've done this, choose your desired VST instrument in the MIDI Output pop-up menu. The output from the track will then be routed to the selected instrument. Depending on the selected instrument, you may also need to select a MIDI channel for the track.

Basic Cubase SX

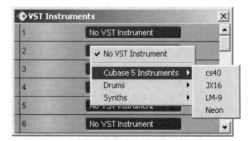

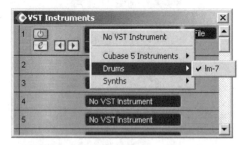

Selecting Cubase 5 instruments (top), drums (middle) and synths (bottom) in Cubase SX

Latency *is a term that describes the length of time it takes for a MIDI instrument to produce a sound when you press a key on your MIDI controller, and it can be a problem with VST instruments. For instance, depending on your audio hardware and its ASIO driver, the latency value may simply be too high to allow comfortable real-time VST instrument playback from your keyboard. However, one way around this problem is to play and record your parts with another MIDI sound source selected and then switch to the VST instrument for playback.*

Drums

Drum sounds are assigned to note values on your MIDI keyboard, as listed below. All mapping is GM-compatible.

DRUM SOUND	NOTE VALUE	COMMENT
Bass	C1	
Rim	C#1	Compressor only
Snare	D1	
Clap	D#1	909 only
Hi-Hat	F#1	
Open Hi-Hat	A#1	
Tom 1	A1	
Tom 2	B2	
Tom 3	D2	

DRUM SOUND	NOTE VALUE	COMMENT
Crash	C#2	
Ride	D#2	Compressor only
Tambourine	F#2	Percussion only
Cowbell	G#2	Percussion only
Hi Bongo	C3	Percussion only
Lo Bongo	C3#	Percussion only
Conga Mute	D3	Percussion only
Conga Open	D#3	Percussion only
Conga Lo	E3	Percussion only
Timbale Lo	G3	Percussion only
Timbale Hi	G#3	Percussion only
Cabasa	A3	Percussion only

VST Effects

Cubase SX also boasts a range of new – or, at least, newly licensed – VST effects bundled for your producing pleasure. These include plug-ins such as DeEsser, Reverb A, Step File and the ubiquitous Vocoder.

DeEsser

A de-esser is used to reduce excessive sibilance, primarily on vocal recordings, so that your singer doesn't end up sounding like Gollum drooling on and on about his precioussssss. Essentially, a de-esser is a special type of compressor that's tuned to be sensitive to the frequencies produced by the 's' sound, hence

SPL DeEsser VST plug-in

the name. Close-proximity microphone placement, pop shields and EQ can help you get the overall sound just right, but depending on the diction of your vocalist, you could still end up with a problem with sibilance. Conventional compression and/or equalising may not easily solve this problem, but a de-esser can.

Reverb A

Reverberation is often used to add ambience and a sense of space to recordings and is probably one of the most important and most commonly used effects in popular and vocal-driven music. Reverb A is a Cubase SX reverb plug-in which provides your recordings with smooth, dense reverb effects. Although this product is new to the PC, a similar plug-in called Reverb 32 did

Reverb A VST plug-in

appear in the previous Mac version of Cubase, VST/32. You can get some particularly nice effects on both vocals and instrumentals with this new plug-in, but keep in mind that reverb, like all effects, should be used sparingly.

StepFilter

StepFilter provides you with a pattern-controlled multimode filter that can create rhythmic, pulsating filter effects and produce two simultaneous 16-step patterns for the filter cut-off and resonance parameters, synchronised to the tempo of the sequencer. You can

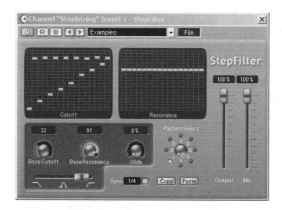

StepFilter VST plug-in

set step values manually by clicking in the pattern-grid windows, and individual step entries can be freely dragged up or down the vertical axis or directly set by clicking in an empty grid box. By click-dragging left or right, consecutive step entries will be set to the pointer position. The higher up the vertical axis a step value is entered, the higher the relative filter cut-off frequency or filter resonance setting. When you start to play back and edit the patterns for the cut-off and resonance parameters of the filter, you can hear precisely how your patterns affect the sound source connected to StepFilter directly.

Vocoder

Through the rather dubious experimentation that went on in the world of '80s pop, most of us now know all too well what a vocoder is. The question is, do we have the good sense not to use it? A vocoder works by applying sound or voice characteristics taken from one signal source, called the *modulator*, and applying them to another source, called the *carrier*. A typical application of a vocoder is to use a voice as a modulator and an instrument as a carrier, making the instrument 'talk'. A vocoder works by dividing the source signal (the modulator) into a number of frequency bands so that the audio attributes of these individual frequency bands can be used to modulate the carrier.

Vocoder VST plug-in

pop-up menu and select 'No Effect'. It's always a good idea to keep this setting for all effects that you don't intend to use in order to minimise processor load.

There are also eight master effect slots available in a separate window or from the Master section in the extended Mixer. When you select and activate master effects, either select the Extended mode for the Mixer and show the Master section or pull down the Devices menu and select 'VST Master Effects' to bring up the Master Effect window, then pull down the pop-up menu for one of the master-effect slots and select an effect.

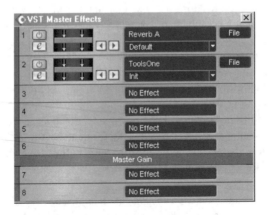

The 'VST Master Effects' dialog box

To change the settings of the effect, click the Edit button to bring up its control panel and similarly, as described above, to turn off a master effect select 'No Effect' for the corresponding slot. Note that master-effect plug-ins must be at least stereo in/out, so if you find you have a plug-in in your 'VSTplugins' folder that you can't assign as a master effect, the reason is probably that it's a mono plug-in.

Accessing VST Instruments

Earlier, I mentioned briefly how to access VST instruments, but to fully activate and play them you'll need to pull down the Devices menu and select 'VST Instruments' from the VST Instruments panel which appears, complete with 32 slots. Next, pull down the pop-up menu for an empty slot in the panel and select your desired instrument. You'll then need to select an unused MIDI track in the Project window and pull down the Output pop-up menu for the MIDI track in the Track list or in the Inspector. This menu will now contain an additional item with the name of the activated VST instrument. Select the VST instrument on the MIDI Output pop-up menu and the MIDI output from the track will be routed to the selected instrument.

Depending on the selected instrument, you may also need to select a MIDI channel for the track, so always check the instrument's documentation for details on its MIDI implementation. Now make sure that 'MIDI Thru Active' is activated in the Preferences dialog and click on the Monitor button for the MIDI track in the Track list, Inspector or Mixer. When this is activated, or when the track is record enabled, incoming MIDI is passed on to the selected MIDI Output, which in this case is the VST instrument.

Now, if you open the Mixer, you'll find an additional channel strip for the instrument's audio outputs. Notice that VST instrument channel strips have the same features and functionality as group-channel strips, with the addition of an Edit (e) button at the top of the strip for opening the VST Instrument control panel. You can use the pop-ups at the bottom of the channel strips to route the instrument audio to the desired output or group and then, *voilà*, you can play the instrument from your MIDI keyboard. You can now also use the Mixer settings to adjust the sound, add EQ or effects, etc, just as with regular audio channels. Of course, you can also record or manually create MIDI parts that play back sounds from the VST instrument if you want to. A word of warning, though: while Cubase SX allows you to have up to 32 VST instruments activated at the same time, software synthesisers can consume quite a lot of processor power, so it's always a good idea to keep an

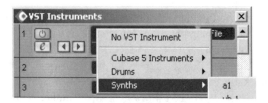

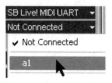

Selecting VST instruments from the VST Instruments dialog box (above) and the Project window (below)

eye on the VST Performance window to avoid running out of steam at a crucial moment.

TIP

While everyone agrees that Cubase SX is now a great deal better at automatically compensating for latency when plug-ins are used as insert effects on audio tracks, this is still not necessarily true for group channels, VST instrument channels or ReWire channels. With this in mind, you should use the VST Dynamics plug-in only as an insert effect for audio-track channels, and possibly as a master effect, if you're using only a single stereo-output bus.

Additional Plug-ins

Apart from the new and newly licensed set of plug-ins featured in Cubase SX, in order to ensure compatibility with songs created in previous versions of Cubase, Steinberg has included most of the previous standard set of VST plug-ins. These include old favourites with colourful names such as Chorus, Phaser, Overdrive, Chopper, Metalizer and Grungelizer, while also included is the more prosaically named but very useful Dynamics.

Chorus

This adds a short delay to the signal and pitch-modulates the delayed signal to produce a doubling effect. It's often a nice effect to be used on acoustic instruments, particularly guitars and strings, or for rounding out pad sounds. If you don't overdo it, chorus can create an illusion of movement and help you build a front-to-back perspective in the mix. However, it does detune your sound a bit, and it can also get a bit samey if it's too strong and can push sounds further back in a mix.

Phaser

Unlike the classic *Star Trek* weapon that can be set to stun or kill, the Phaser plug-in produces the classic swooshing sound immortalised in stunning iconic rock tracks such as The Small Faces' 'Itchycoo Park' and Status Quo's nearly credible 'Pictures Of Matchstick

Men'. (Just kidding about the 'stunning' and 'iconic', by the way.) Of course, this effect has been used in many different ways by many different artists. It works by shifting the phase of a signal and adding the result back to the original signal, causing partial cancellation of the frequency spectrum. It's very good for pads, but it can muddy a mix if over-used. Use it effectively in combination with other effects.

Overdrive

Overdrive is a distortion-type effect that emulates the sound of a guitar amplifier. There's a selection of factory styles available and none of these are stored parameter settings but different basic overdrive algorithms. Like Distortion, the characteristics of the styles found on the Overdrive plug-in are indicated by their names, and this effect could be helpful if you wanted to sound like the late great Jerry Garcia or the even later and greater Jimi Hendrix.

Chopper

With no connection whatsoever to a Harley Davidson or Easy Rider, Chopper2 is an effect that uses different waveforms to modulate the level (tremolo) or left-right stereo position (pan) of a signal, either using the Tempo Sync facility or manual modulation-speed settings. It can be used to produce tremolo-style effects and can also produce autopan effects when set to stereo. It livens up synth sounds and works well with a flanger.

Metalizer

The Metalizer plug-in feeds an audio signal through a variable-frequency filter, applying Tempo Sync or time modulation and feedback control. If you're a fan of Ozzie and the crew, this is great if you're looking for that Aerosmith or Black Sabbath sound.

Grungelizer

This adds noise and static to your recordings, producing sounds like those produced by an old radio with bad reception or a worn and scratched vinyl record. It's great for use with beats, samples and for remixes, or for artificially ageing a sound, and it can also be used with other effects to create an absolutely filthy guitar sound.

VST Dynamics

You can radically alter the dynamic range or level of audio material in Cubase SX with the built-in dynamic processor. Each audio channel has its own 'VST Dynamics' section, and this panel gives you access to AutoGate, AutoLevel, Compress, SoftClip and Limit processors. When you click on one or more of the processor label buttons, the dynamic is inserted after any regular insert effects and before the EQ section and channel fader.

So what do these weird processor names actually do? Well, compared to plain vanilla dynamics, VST Dynamics has two additional modules called AutoLevel and SoftClip. The signal flow is fixed, in the order AutoGate-AutoLevel-Compress-SoftClip-Limit. Be aware that VST Dynamics has a higher inherent latency than regular effects, so signals will be delayed when passing through the plug-in. Here's a run-down of the processors' functions:

- **AutoGate** – A noise gate similar to hardware devices found in traditional studios and used for cutting out unwanted signals like noise and interference which may be present between sections wanted material.

- **AutoLevel** – An automatic level control designed to even out signal differences in audio material and to boost low-level signals or attenuate high-level signals.

- **Compress** – Like the standard audio compressors used in traditional studios, this converts loud parts into quieter parts and quiet parts into louder parts.

- **SoftClip** – This is like an automatic gain control which you can't really adjust. It's designed to keep sounds within certain decibel parameters and create a warmer, valve-amp-style sound.

- **Limit** – This performs the same role as a hardware limiter and is generally used to stop an output signal from passing above a set threshold, no matter how loud the input becomes.

Summary

VST instruments and plug-ins are being aggressively marketed as convenient, cheap alternatives to the usual range of expensive hardware synths, samplers and rack effects, and for the most part they probably are. However, they still take up a huge amount of memory and will ravenously devour whatever processing power you have available. Plug-in effects normally provide fairly trouble-free performance, although some of them can introduce a slight delay to an audio signal.

That said, VST instruments can save you loads of money on more expensive hardware synths, although they may not be as convenient to use, depending on your style of music and playing. And before you use any effect in your music, it's probably worth asking yourself, 'Why?' – or, perhaps more specifically, 'Is this really necessary?' VST makes effects so easy to use that there's always the temptation to over-use them just because you can. Remember that effects are there to create an illusion, so don't let them become delusions.